MW00563445

SEEN AND (UN) HEARD

A Little Girl's Journey
From Silence To Empowerment

PATRICIA LOVE

DEDICATION

This book is dedicated to the two souls that came together and gave me the strength to write this book and help me thrive again.

To my angel, my sister, Ginger who mentored me from the time I was born, until her last very breath. You gave me hope and courage. You inspired me in life, and in death. You taught me how to blow smoke rings (which makes me laugh to this day), and how to play a good game of gin rummy. And for all that and more, I love you beyond what words could possibly express.

To Hula, my cat of 18 years who was so much more than a cat. You had such a deep empathic soul, which crossed the boundaries of the Universe and broke all cosmic rules, leading me to find the inner peace that I have today.

And last by not least, to all the little girls growing up around the world. You deserve to be seen and heard because you exist, nothing more. And in the moments where you feel confused, scared or lost, know that you are never alone. Although we don't know each other, I see you and I'm listening. And I know there are others out there waiting to hear your courageous voice speak. You are worthy and enough, and I can't wait to witness all of your beautiful self-expression unfold, in one way or another. The world needs you. Just as you are.

ACKNOWLEDGEMENT

I want to thank my Book Writing Mentor and Editor, Sheree Trask for holding my hand throughout the writing process, encouraging me to be vulnerable, and showing me the power of being brave to create space for the words to flow from my heart onto the pages.

TABLE OF CONTENTS

INTRODUCTION

"You've always had the power, my dear,
you just had to learn it yourself."

- Wizard of Oz

The answer is yes, you *are* in the right place. How do I know this? Because there is a specific reason you picked up this book, at this particular moment, at this particular time in your life. There are no coincidences, only Universal interventions, and I truly believe that your journey is unfolding in Divine timing. I also believe there's always a purpose and that every piece of your story has been placed perfectly to serve the highest and best expression of YOU.

This is a choice point for you. You can choose to stay in your comfort zone and let life happen as it's been happening… Or, you can take a step forward and move into the unknown, grounding into the intention that this next chapter will not only be incredible, but it will be the best chapter you've experienced thus far.

Right now, as you read this, you may be experiencing anxiety, stress, maybe even fear because you're not where you thought you'd be in your life at this point. Maybe you're having sleepless nights, finding your mind wandering and questioning yourself, asking things like: *What's missing? Why do I feel so empty? Why am I not happy?*

The good news is, you have the power to change those thoughts and feelings and in doing so, you can change your life *for good!*

I know it's not easy to change, and I know all too well that it may feel easier to stay right where you are, even though you may not be happy. The comfortability of the path you're on feels safe because it's familiar, which makes sense! But if you're not enjoying the ride, what's the point?

This might be hard to hear, but I'm not here to sugarcoat things. I'm here to share the truth so that you can decide (or not) to do something differently and finally step into the life waiting for you. By staying complacent, what you're really saying to yourself is, "I'm comfortable (and okay) with being unhappy." And as much as I'm sure you're hesitant to own that responsibility, trust me when I say, I understand (because I've been there, too) - and change is possible.

It's not always easy to look ourselves in the mirror and admit that maybe, just maybe, we're not as perfect as we'd hoped we'd appear to the outside world (or to ourselves). But by ignoring the signals that are encouraging us to shift, we are choosing to remain where we're at, leaving joy and fulfillment on the table.

The saying, 'no risk, no reward' is true. And if that scares you, that's okay! It scared me for years, until I decided that I had nothing (literally) left to lose.

Keeping your mind healthy is a necessity, and it takes courage to start that process of truth and self-reflection in order to acknowledge your negative thoughts and real-life situations. And although it may feel uncomfortable in the moment, the courage necessary to change already resides within you. If you know in your heart that it's time to make some changes because what you're doing right now isn't working (not fully, at least), then I am here to encourage and empower you to do just that. It's time to harness your brave spirit and lean into that fear so that you can be free to live and experience life and all it has to offer.

Owning up to one's own truth is arguably one of the hardest (and bravest) things you can do. And believe me, if you're struggling to lean into the discomfort and uproot all that you know to gain more of what you desire, I get it! Taking a look in the mirror and consciously witnessing ourselves can be incredibly uncomfortable and massively confronting! But in doing so, we open ourselves to the opportunity to experience more pleasure and abundance in all areas of our lives.

Sounds pretty great, right?

THE SMOKESCREEN OF PERFECTION

For a long time my life looked perfect to the outside world. My friends thought I had it all - the money, the cars, the career... the epitome of a happy life. And from the outside, it was true! I was all laughter and smiles in public. Meanwhile, I was covering up the fact that I felt empty and alone inside, and was seeking love and happiness in all the wrong places. I was placing all my negative thoughts, past traumas, setbacks, and anxieties into my internal suitcase that kept expanding and getting heavier by the day. I lugged that baggage around with me everywhere I went, and as it got heavier and harder to carry, I found ways to appear stronger just so I could cover up the truth of what was really going on underneath my many masks.

I covered my pain with lipstick to make me feel better. And although temporarily, it did help me feel lighter in the midst of the madness. Honestly, I never stopped to think about what was happening, and I sure as shit didn't want to dive in and figure out why I was feeling the way I did. All I knew was that I wanted the pain to disappear, so I hid my truth from myself and everyone else, using drugs, booze, men, and money to mask all the hidden pain and trauma I'd yet to address.

I was busting my ass to prove to the world that I belonged. If I could just be pretty enough, smart enough, rich enough, funny enough... they would love me. And even when I did begin to feel worthy or enough, the feelings were short-lived and always, I was left empty.

I now know that the real fear was coming face to face with the truth of my soul, a dark and scary place that I'd never allowed myself to experience. And while there was no way in hell I was going to admit it back then, the truth was, I was an imposter. For others to see the real me, and know this deep, dark secret was the biggest fear of my life. And something I knew I'd have to face at some point.

I wanted people to believe I was perfect. And although intellectu-ally I knew that was an impossible ideal to live up to, I did not have the emotional courage or strength to expose myself for the woman I'd become in the process of hiding. The idea of opening up in that way, and being seen naked in my truth made me want to throw up. It felt too vulnerable, too real, too… *final*. I liked the facade I'd been living under. I didn't want to give up this mask I'd been wearing for decades. But at the same time, I was tired, and I knew I couldn't continue going on this way any longer.

NEVER ALONE

If any of this sounds like your story, know that you're not alone. And if you feel hopeless, like I did, also know that anything is possible and you are now, and always have been, worthy of living a life you love.

This is not just another book to leave on your bookshelf to collect dust. This book is an invitation into the next chapter of your life. And if you allow it to, this book could very well be the missing link you've been waiting for to realize that you're not broken, life is not over for you, and yes, there is so much more available.

And this is not just another book to inspire your greatness, either. I have taken my decades of failures, and paired them with real life successes in a memoir of sorts to save you time in the process of your own transformation as you reclaim your power, and take back what's yours - YOUR LIFE!

Think about the happiness, pure joy, and all the dreams that filled your mind when you were young. *That little girl still lives within you.* In fact, she's in all of us! But somehow, over time she became quieter and quieter, and somewhere along the way, we stopped listening to her whispers, shutting down her dreams and aspirations in the process. All of the excitement that little girl once felt to be a vet, a doctor, a singer, even the President - shattered. All because the adult version of us said there wasn't time, we weren't enough, it was impossible, it wasn't important -- or whatever other bullshit story we chose to make us feel better about quitting on ourselves!

Bottom line: we trampled all over that little girl's dreams and stopped honoring our hearts deepest desires for no other reason than we were *scared of our own power.*

The thing is, that little girl inside of you is still very much alive. And despite the outside chatter of the world telling her why she was wrong, bad, or whatever other completely false stories she heard, and ultimately chose to believe, she (you) has always been worthy and enough. You've got all the power you need within. Strapped with that truth, now it's about granting yourself permission to come back home to yourself, and honoring your inner child, once and for all.

Any doubts you've had, whether from society, family, or even yourself - all of that changes now. Because that little girl that's been hiding inside has the qualities, capabilities, and the power to control and write her own destiny from this point forward. There's no reason to wait any longer to become all of you. In case you needed it, this is your permission to stand tall in your brilliance as the beautiful woman that you are.

You are unique and a gift to this world in every way. And I know that the idea of loving yourself completely might feel uncomfortable, but there's power in the willingness to shed the layers and step into your rawness as you embrace more love and compassion for yourself, and your journey. By loving yourself, the negativity in the world becomes more of a whisper than a shout, and you realize that even the weight of everything outside of you cannot penetrate your own personal power or love for the woman you are, and the little girl that will always live within your being. It's work, and it doesn't happen overnight. But it's possible to change, and when it happens, you'll realize just how beautiful life can be when you allow yourself to be all of you... complete with your little girl dreams and all.

While this book may be written using my personal stories as examples, it's not actually about me at all. It's about uncovering the masks that we all wear to protect, distract and avoid our own personal truth. It's about taking your internal power back, and honoring your needs. It's about uncovering the stories and patterns that led you to focus so much of your energy on pleasing others before yourself.

We're all so much more similar than we'd like to admit. And as I tell my stories throughout these pages, I have no doubt that they will open you up to your own stories as well - the ones that you might have stuffed into your own suitcase in hopes of hiding the pain, sadness, grief, shame, guilt, and anything else that's prevented you from shining your bright light all these years.

WHAT TO EXPECT

At the end of each chapter, I will give you a question to ponder to help you change any negative or unsupportive behaviors so that you can finally begin to open your heart, and remember what it feels like to embody the innocence of your inner child. At one point, she was free and fierce and wildly optimistic. <u>She is you, and that hasn't changed.</u>

The examples and questions I share throughout these pages are the very tools that I used to change my own behaviors as well as my perspectives in life. They allowed me to open myself up in ways that invited in more abundance and love, which opened me up to the life waiting for me underneath my 'everything's fine' exterior. I want to encourage you to use these tools, and give yourself permission to begin to live from your soul, which is where you'll find not only your inner power, but your inner peace and the joy you've been seeking (likely outside of yourself) for far too long.

This is the beginning of your new story, the one that you've consciously chosen to write from a place of **empowerment and love**. This is your invitation to awaken your awareness, begin a new chapter, and create a life full of more happiness, more love, and more success in whatever capacity you choose.

And even if it feels scary to dive in, I want you to know that although these are merely words on a page to you right now, I can feel your rise and I believe in your ability to rekindle your own power. You might not feel ready, but I know that you are. You picked up this book after all, didn't you? That tells me that somewhere inside, your soul is asking for permission to try something new so here it is.

I'm so proud of your courage.

I have written this book for the little girl within us all, and to the little girls that have preceded us, as well as those that will come after us. We all have the power to rise, do and become anything our heart desires, no matter where you happen to be in life. It's time to step into your power and own it with reckless abandon. It does not matter your age, your environment, or your situation - you got this!

And I've got you!

1

TOO PRETTY TO SPEAK

The Swing

How do you like to go up in a swing,
Up in the air so blue?
Oh, I do think it the pleasantest thing
Ever a child can do!

Up in the air and over the wall,
Till I can see so wide,
Rivers and trees and cattle and all
Over the countryside—

Till I look down on the garden green,
Down on the roof so brown—
Up in the air I go flying again,
Up in the air and down!

- Robert Louis Stevenson

One of my fondest childhood memories was when my older sister, Ginger (who was 14 at the time, and 10 years my senior) taught me how to swing. She would say, "Patty, put your legs straight out when I push you forward and then fold them back under you when you come back in. You can do it!" We would giggle and laugh as I tried my best to go faster and faster and higher and higher. I didn't understand the symbolism of freedom that the swing had at the time, but when I was 4, I knew being on it felt good and it made me very happy.

When I found the poem, 'The Swing' many years later in my teens, it became a treasure in my life. I memorized it, and thought about it often, especially when I felt upset, stressed or alone. I would sit back and imagine myself on that swing, going up in the air, flying oh so high, free of worry, and feeling like I could do anything. I felt truly unstoppable.

It's so interesting how we begin to adopt doubt as we get older. As children, we're born into this world so pure and fearless and somewhere along the way, our perception changes. When we're young, it's normal (even acceptable) to believe in Unicorns, and the thought of traveling across rainbows into different galaxies not only seemed simple, but completely realistic.

Think back to your own childhood. That unstoppable feeling that swirled around in the deepest part of your being, fueling the belief that the world was your playground meant to be explored and experienced. Your excitement was contagious as you went about your days touching the depths of life, eyes wide with your heart expanded, totally open.

You were free, until life told you that you weren't, making you believe that you needed to be somebody other than yourself. Whether through personal experience, or adopting other people's fears and limitations, or witnessing the failures of the world through your very own innocent eyes, you began to retract and before you knew it, your dreams seemed out of reach. Maybe even crazy.

THE MOMENT THAT CHANGED EVERYTHING

I remember it as if it were yesterday...

I was a precocious child - outspoken, energetic, always smiling, and full of life. Until the age of 3, when all of that changed. I'll never forget the day, for this particular event was etched like stone into my memory, where it's lived ever since.

I vividly remember skipping down the street in downtown Spokane, WA in my pretty pink dress holding tight to Mary, my new Tiny Tears doll that I'd gotten for my birthday. It was a warm Summer day and above all else, I was deeply happy.

My mom, sister and I were holding hands as we skipped and sang our hearts out down that tree-lined street, seemingly without a care in the world, when an older African-American woman stopped us. As she looked down at me, I could feel my cheeks flush...

"What a beautiful child you have... so very pretty!" she said. "Thank you! Did you notice my very long eyelashes?" I replied. Followed innocently by, "why are you so black?"

Kids certainly do say what's on their mind, and I was no different. Thankfully, instead of being offended, the woman graciously smiled and let me know that yes, she had noticed my pretty eyelashes, and the color of her skin? "Well, I was born this way, just like you were born with pretty lashes." As you might imagine, my mom was horrified. I was taught to be polite and to always respect my elders but in this moment, it became clear as day that I was completely out of line, and my mother made sure I knew so.

That seemingly innocent chain of events was a pivotal moment that changed everything for me. As my mother kneeled down and looked into my eyes, she pointed her finger in my face in disbelief at what had just come out of my mouth and declared, "Little girls are to be seen, and not heard, young lady! Know your place, and don't embarrass me again!"

My big, innocent eyes filled with tears and as they began to roll down my cheeks, I promised my mother it would never happen again. Even at 3 years old, I knew I'd done something "wrong" and while it wasn't ill-intended, I also knew that I never wanted to hurt my mother. Yet here I was, ruining a perfect afternoon by speaking 'out of line' while being given a lesson in silencing myself to appease the comfort of others.

My mom was angry with me for the entire car ride home. She threatened not to take me anywhere ever again unless I learned to "act right." My sister was the quiet one, but was always there to console me. And as she put her arm around me in the backseat of our white,

1953 Mercury 2-door coupe, I could feel the words she'd neglected to say aloud, promising me that it was going to be okay. I sunk into her embrace, so grateful to have her, my sister, my protector, and forever my biggest cheerleader.

That was the longest car ride of my young life, and as I held tightly onto my doll, I contemplated what had just happened, all the while confused as to what it was that I did wrong. The story I made up was that using my voice meant I was bad and from that point forward, I became a different version of myself, constantly worried about what others might think if I spoke up and allowed myself to be heard.

Take a moment and think back to a memory in your past that helped shape you -- good, bad, or indifferent. Who were you with? How old were you? What happened? What is the belief or story that shifted because of it? How has it followed you all these years later? Is it serving your highest good, or keeping you stuck in the past?

You see, we all have patterns, and they weren't created out of nowhere. Somewhere along the way, we had an experience that asked us to choose a belief based on the feeling we had in that particular moment. And for many of us, we have carried them with us for years, maybe even decades, hiding pieces of our truth in the process.

It is the continued small (and large) events that happen to us as children that help shape us as we become adults, leaving lasting effects which often change how we view the world. I certainly didn't start out shy or hiding behind my mom's skirt when people spoke. But after that incident on the street, and more of these "only speak when spoken to" events happened throughout my life, I became more reclusive, more tentative, more introverted, and scared to say the wrong thing.

THE POWER OF WORDS

This is just one of the ways our innocence begins to diminish. We're told by someone we perceive as 'important' or 'powerful' what to do, what to say, how to act, and over time, the shaming or silencing of our truth breaks us down. At first, these kinds of statements may seem small, and you might even try to shrug them off. But words matter, and whether intentionally or not, they leave imprints that can build us up, or tear us down. Words hold power. And the wrong kind of language from someone we admire, or even a stranger on the street, or another kid on the playground can lead to the little girl within ourselves to shrink, and silence, losing her voice and feeling afraid to be seen (and heard) even decades later.

All of these unintentionally discouraging statements we're told, or even those we overhear as children, are the very things that lead to confusion. We stack them one on top of the other and hold onto them as if they're true, contributing to a belief that says we're not enough, and it's better that we keep our mouths shut to avoid embarrassing someone, or saying the wrong thing.

I'm willing to bet that most women who read this book have had their own "innocent stranger discrimination" moment like I did. Something that occurred that took you from confident, fearless, and vibrant to apprehensive, guarded, and uncertain. The thing is, our mind is so intelligent. And it will believe whatever we tell it! That is why it's so important to feed ourselves nourishing thoughts to support the feelings we want to have in order to create the life we want to live. But as children, we don't know any better. Not yet, anyway.

GROWING PAINS

As the years went by, the constant reminder to *shut up, do as you're told,* and *don't speak unless spoken to* continued. I would hide out in my bedroom where I could be alone without worrying about messing up. I would play music, and snuggle with my cat, Gina, who was not allowed in the house (although I always snuck her in anyway). This seemed to calm me, as I listened to the words of the music and dreamt of faraway places, tucked away in the safety of my room until it was time for dinner.

Dinner was a whole production in my house. Under no circumstances could you ever be late, especially if my father was home (he traveled a lot for work), which brought an entirely different energy to our household.

I could feel myself getting more and more frustrated each day, feeling like I could never do anything right. My nightly school work became harder and harder, and frustration would set in when the things I was working so hard on didn't lead to my definition of success. Instead, I felt like a total failure in life and as though I would never be smart enough to achieve my goals and dreams. And to make matters worse, the criticism from my mom when comparing me to my brother, who was 7 years older than me, didn't help. She'd say things like, "you're not that stupid..." or "be more like your brother, he's smart..." which was understandably discouraging to hear, and definitely a blow to my already dwindling self-esteem.

This communication became normal in our household. When my father would take us all out to dinner, or on any outing where there might be other people involved, I was continuously reminded not to speak or fidget and instead, to just "sit and look pretty." I was warned that making a scene of any kind would lead to repercussions when I got home, so I learned very early on to stay quiet, and still.

I had remembered how my older brother and sister had gotten spanked with my dad's leather belt several times when they acted out, and I didn't want that to happen to me. I learned quickly that it was best to stay on the good side of my father, and follow his rules. The truth was, life at home was much easier and less complicated when he was away, although I missed him terribly when he was gone.

THE NEW GIRL

I remember being 10 years old and starting 5th grade in a brand new school... a week late, which is rarely an easy transition for any kid. We had moved from a rental into my dad's dream home in a very upscale neighborhood, far different from what I'd come to know growing up. I remember walking into class, and the teacher making me stand in front of everyone to tell the class who I was and where I was from. I could feel all eyes on me and all I wanted to do was shrink into the background and hide. I could hear their whispers about me, which made me feel insecure and unwelcomed. Being new at any age can be tough, but as a child, it can be straight torture to feel different and unliked by your peers. I was always ignored during lunch and ended up eating alone most days, praying for the end of school bell so I could run home and hide in my room with my cat and my music.

Over the next few months I tolerated the girls at school. And even though I was not allowed in their group, I pretended that it didn't bother me. All the while, on the inside, I was aching to be wanted, and included. During this time, one of the popular boys, Kirk befriended me, and we started hanging out pretty regularly. When he asked me to go steady, I was ecstatic! I was only in 5th grade, but as the new girl in school with no friends, having one of the most popular boys ask me to be his girlfriend felt like a huge deal. I was giddy with joy, and finally felt special and accepted, even if those feelings were coming from a young boy that I barely knew.

But that happiness didn't last more than a few days. Just as I was settling into my new normal, one of the 'mean' girls who didn't like me started a terrible rumor that in order to go steady with Kirk, I had demanded that he buy me a stereo set (which was completely false). At that young and impressionable age, it felt like my world was ending. People began talking behind my back, making up stories about me, and although he knew better, Kirk began to believe the lies. Not only was I humiliated, but Kirk ended up breaking up with me and I went back to being the unpopular new girl that nobody seemed to like.

I found myself alone once again. I felt like I couldn't do anything right, so I decided that I would do whatever I had to do not to go back to school. Because when you're 10 years old, that seems totally reasonable.

The rumors had upset me so much that I lied to my mom and told her I didn't feel good so she would let me stay home. I even got sneaky and started putting the thermometer under hot water before she would take my temperature - and it worked! I continued to have a temperature for almost two weeks just to stay out of school. That is, until my mom said she was taking me to the doctor, which put an end to my charade pretty quickly, and I couldn't fake the sickness anymore.

When I went back to school, I pretended that I wasn't hurt by their actions, and refused to show my true emotions for fear of appearing weak. I was frightened to tell my mom about the bullying for if I did, I knew she would tell my dad, and I would have gotten the belt for going steady with a boy. I was too scared to cause more trouble so instead, I remained silent like a "good girl."

I was nervous to go back to school so I told myself to just ignore those mean girls and keep my distance and by doing so, everything would be fine. Some of the girls still bullied me a bit for a while, but I continued to keep to myself. I remained strong and kept a stiff upper lip, and since I didn't get angry and they couldn't get me to fight back, eventually they moved on to bully someone else. I learned that by having a flippant attitude, showing strength on the outside, and not letting anyone in, I could avoid being hurt. I was learning to hide my vulnerabilities, which is how I survived. I was getting really good at faking it to the outside world, all while my little 10 year old self was crying inside, dying to feel accepted and loved.

When I wasn't at school, I found happiness on the swing, or laying on the grass at night looking up at the millions of stars. These things became my escape and for the smallest of moments, I believed that someday, someone would see that I mattered and love all of me, as I was.

IMPRINTS

Because of the bullying at such a young age, and constantly hearing belittling words at home, that outgoing, precocious little girl became an introvert. I found myself wanting to please everyone, so I would put a smile on my face and act like nothing was wrong. Over and over again, this method of hiding my truth proved to work and I noticed that the more agreeable I was (especially to my parents), the easier life seemed to be.

My father was a traveling salesperson and my mom worked for my father in his office as his secretary. I was what they called back then a "latch key kid," coming home from school every day to an empty home, making my own meals, and sometimes, putting myself to bed. My parents never pushed or inspired me to do or be anything, and

I was never acknowledged for anything good that I did anyway. So instead of trying to impress my parents, I did nothing. I was a young girl, simply existing in a big, scary, (and by all accounts) mean world.

When she was home, my mother always told me to get out of the house. I rarely brought friends home because of the way she would act. I always knew something was different about her, but I didn't know what, exactly.

And then there was my father. When he was around, the only thing we ever seemed to do was negotiate with one another. Like if my grades were good, he would buy me things or give me money or take me on trips. He would also put me on display by acting as the cute bartender for him and his friends, or faking that I could play the organ through his electrical genius. This was the only way I felt I could get his attention so I held onto it tightly. I learned to negotiate my allowance, chores and anything else just to make him happy. He would call me his little salesman, which I guess in some ways paid off later in life. What I really wanted though, was his love. The material things were fillers for the longing I felt within, which I never expressed.

My Sister, My Angel

I had two best friends from the neighborhood that I played with, along with my older sister, who always wanted to protect me. I looked up to her so much. From the beginning, she took me under her wing and even though I didn't understand it, I could feel her love and protection, which lasted until her death many years later. I gravitated towards her and wanted to be around her as much as possible. She had a way of making me feel secure and safe in her presence, something I craved to feel with my parents and could never quite grasp. She would take me places, and talk to me, always making sure I was okay. I just thought she was being a good older sister, which she was! But it wasn't until my late teens that I really understood why she has always been so nurturing towards me.

Over the years the light I'd once had began to dim, and it showed. But when I was with my sister, it's like the light switch was turned back on and I found myself feeling happy and free. In her presence,

I never felt judged, or criticized. In fact, I felt the complete opposite. She would always build me up, smiling at me with her crooked smile, something that we joked about. She told me I was a gift and that she understood how hard it was to live in the house, but not to give up. She was my only real lifeline growing up, and I loved her deeply for it.

Some of my favorite times with my sister were at night when I was 10, 11 and 12 years old, before she moved out of the house. I would sneak downstairs to her bedroom on a regular basis after my parents went to bed. We would play cards - usually rummy, and poker. She even taught me how to smoke and blow smoke rings (in retrospect, maybe not the best thing to be teaching me, especially as a kid). She would tell me all about her boyfriends and I truly believed that she could do no wrong. I idolized her, and I wanted to be just like her.

Teenage years are hard enough, but I couldn't shake the feeling of loneliness. I felt lost, with no sense of purpose or meaning. My friends all had goals, like becoming teachers, nurses, or moms. I had none of those. I had so many different and confusing messages coming at me from my parents and teachers, and up to this point, I hadn't been given any direction, inspiration or discipline.

I was basically left to indulge myself in whatever I felt like, which to a child, can be detrimental. Charging things on my mom's Nordstrom account, always having cash… that was normal for me. When I was old enough to drive, my mother was thrilled, and gave me her blue 1968 Mustang convertible to use anytime I wanted. I would even pick her up from work sometimes, which made me feel special. I became the driver for all my friends because none of their parents allowed them to use their cars like mine did. I felt like I was somebody, no longer invisible, yet still overcome with a sense of emptiness and a yearning for more.

Having a car gave me a feeling of freedom, escapism, and pro-vided a moment where everything felt right. Very much the way I remembered feeling as a kid being on that swing, or looking at the stars. I felt important, and finally, in control.

As far as school, I was never a good student like my friends. I was smart, but nothing interested me, so I didn't apply myself. I continued to showcase my upbeat personality to the outside world, hoping they wouldn't pry and ask questions. But it was all a cover up. When I was alone, things would go back to normal, which for me meant sadness, loneliness, and a feeling of being disconnected from myself and those around me.

One day I was in my dad's office and found a book called, "Think and Grow Rich" by Napoleon Hill. I was fascinated by the words in the title and began to read through the book ferociously. It held my interest and opened my mind up to the idea that there was hope. I held onto that book, trying to understand the positive words and figure out how I could implement them into my life. *"Whatever the mind of man can conceive and believe, it can achieve."* I didn't realize the impact that those words would have on my life until years later when things as I knew it would change once again.

In my teens, I developed a slight stutter. I couldn't think fast enough on my feet, so when people would ask me questions, especially if I was put on the spot, criticized or asked about something I didn't understand, it was hard for me to think of the right words to say. Because of this, I found it hard to listen because I was so focused on being able to respond correctly. I had a tendency to talk over people before they were finished speaking, which frustrated everyone involved, myself included.

I had a fear of deep conversations because of this causing me to stay on the surface in all of my communication. My words didn't flow easily, so I would sit back and again, practice being silent, just like I did as a little girl. People thought I was charming and engaging because I had taught myself when to smile and laugh at all the right times. But all that surface talk to get by created a fear within me of going deeper, and letting people get to know more about me. If I stayed in my own bubble, nobody could hurt me. Maybe I wouldn't receive love, that was true. But more importantly, I wouldn't have to feel ashamed or criticized for being who I was.

I was a bit of a late bloomer and as I matured, and moved into my mid to late teenage years, the "baby weight" dropped off and my body blossomed. A lot of people called me very pretty, and boys were interested in me, but the messages I kept getting became more confusing than ever, especially from my father. He would constantly

11

PATRICIA LOVE

tell me that men could not be trusted, that they just wanted to take advantage of young girls like myself, and I needed to be careful not to get pregnant. I learned to be tough and independent, something I felt I'd been training for my entire life. Then, out of the other side of his mouth he would say things like, "you will make a great wife someday," "you are so pretty... any man would want you."

During that time of mass internal conflict, my parents thought it would be a good idea to put me into modeling school. I was 16, which I guess meant it was time to learn all about etiquette and how to be a proper lady. But all it did was emphasize the fact that I was just a pretty face to look at, while remaining silent to the outside world.

Meanwhile, my much older brother and sister were off to college, something I was never encouraged to pursue. I was told that all I needed was my looks, which for whatever reason could somehow "take me wherever I needed to go." Yet this statement was always accompanied by the reminder not to trust people, especially men, because they would lead me astray.

Why was I so different from my siblings, who both went to college? Did they think I was not smart enough to make it into college? Did they discriminate against me because I was "pretty" and blonde?

If those were in fact their beliefs, then I definitely proved them right. I barely got into a state college and once I did, I flunked out after only a year and half. This confirmed my own belief based on my conditioning that I wasn't good enough, or smart enough. From as far back as I can recall, my life was full of confusion and uncertainty, which left me searching for something I couldn't seem to find - acceptance and love.

WORDS MATTER

My internal compass as to what was 'right' had been muffled by so many opinions I couldn't seem to figure out what it was that I believed. I took the information I was given from words and subsequent actions and formed stories to support my biases. Looking back, I endured quite a bit of mental and emotional chaos, what I now know to be a form of abuse. But growing up, it was simply all I knew.

Often when we hear the word 'abuse,' we think of broken bones and bruises. But mental abuse can be just as, if not more, detrimental long-term. The incessant negative chatter leaves holes in the soul, and becomes what I call, a silent killer of the mind.

In today's world, more than ever, we must choose our words wisely. Instead of putting people down, my hope is to inspire and encourage people to use their words to build people up. We have so much power in the way we speak. I'm proof of that. Maybe you are too.

Of course this is true for all people, but for the intents of this book, I want to focus on little girls. Because I believe they should feel loved and equal in every way from the moment they enter this world. They should understand that they belong, and their words and thoughts matter. They should be told from the start that they are a gift and that their voices bring fresh perspectives to everyday thoughts and challenges that arise in this world. They need to know at a young age that their voice is important and deserves to be heard. They should know they have a light within and the power to do and be whatever they choose.

I know I wish I'd had more of that early on. And because I can't change my past, I made the decision to choose a better future, which meant finding the path home to my truth so that I could finally be free to unfold my soul safely and share all of myself with the world.

This is the time to remind the little girl inside us that no matter what age you may be right now, you are safe, and good enough, and worthy of all the beautiful things in your life. It doesn't matter if you're 16 or 82! The road is paved for safe traveling.

REFLECTION

What is the little girl within saying to you when no one is watching? If your words are unsupportive or out of alignment with how you want to feel inside, are you willing to create a new dialogue?

2

FAKE IT TIL YOU MAKE IT

A chameleon, I change my clothes
Not to mislead or to indulge in deceit
To gauge your needs and mine, to fit in
I use the props that you allotted
Polishing, repairing… learning
My trunks brims, I ask no more

- Eric Alagan

Growing up is hard, and the people that surround us, as we explore our growing pains, are the ones we learn from. Whether that is a parent, a teacher, or family member, they shape our complete childhood experience.

Look back on your own little girl experiences. Did you have times of sadness, longing or feeling less than? Did you feel the need to be compliant or have the aim to please everyone growing up? Were you overlooked or ignored? Maybe you're still struggling (as an adult) to be seen and heard, or constantly doing things in order to validate your worth. Often, these feelings stem from the little girl within that still feels confused based on the conditioning you received from a young age.

14

And although it may feel uncomfortable, it's important to identify and acknowledge the people that helped form your experiences and thoughts as a young girl. Doing so enables you to take back your power so you can move forward and blossom.

The people that shaped me were primarily my parents and my sister. Yours may be your parents, or even an uncle or a friend of the family. Whomever they are, identifying them will help you better understand the impact their role (and their imprints) had on your life. And possibly, the role they continue to play in your life to this day.

Like many little girls, being 'Daddy's Girl' was all I wanted growing up. The feeling of having my father's love and acceptance seemed far fetched, but regardless, it was something I worked hard to attain. I would imagine running into my daddy's arms as I heard him drive up the driveway after he'd been away for a week of work. I would give him a big hug, just like I used to see on the TV shows, as he picked me up in his arms and embraced me like I was the only person that mattered in the world.

Unfortunately, that didn't happen as my dad had learned that in order to forget his own traumatic past of poverty, abuse and (lack of) love, he needed to shut off any of his personal emotions to survive. He felt the need to keep his emotions repressed, never realizing how doing so affected his relationships, primarily the ones with his own children.

My father pushed his story deep within, and only showed his outwardly charismatic demeanor to the public eye. The thought of people knowing that he grew up dirt poor, living in squalor, with holes in his shoes, never knowing if his mother (who was abused by his biological father) would be home to feed him and his younger sisters, horrified him. Because of this, he believed his only alternative was to pretend that none of it had ever happened. He did everything he could to keep his truth buried, as he believed that he would lose respect from his colleagues and family if anyone knew the real backstory.

THE MASK OF SHAME

His emotions had been pushed down so far that years later, he blatantly walked by his own father on the street who was sitting on the ground begging, visibly disheveled, and obviously homeless. My father refused to acknowledge his own father's existence due to the shame he held so close to his heart. To my dad, this homeless man who had been abusive, jailed for murdering an IRS man and who had willingly starved his family was the equivalent of a piece of garbage that had been thrown out and was not deserving of any kindness. Not even from his own son.

My fathers only goal was to elevate himself and rise above his rough beginnings. He believed he was protecting his family, yet his scars were so embedded that they prevented him from having a healthy relationship with his own chosen family (my mother, my siblings, and I).

But as a child, I didn't understand that I saw my dad, who I idolized and looked up to, through the lens of false perception. I saw the side he wanted everyone to see, which was a powerful, appropriate, successful, physically fit, man always strutting around in his custom suits and dress shirts. His ties always matched, and his cufflinks sparkled. He was seemingly perfect in every way (at least externally), all the way down to the matching pocket square in his suit jacket.

This was a man that was outwardly in control, and always controlled the room. But to me, he was just my daddy. And all I wanted was to be his little girl... to be loved and noticed... to run into his arms and hug him and know that I mattered by being hugged back.

You may have had similar feelings growing up within your family. Maybe you grew up as an invisible child. Maybe you needed to learn to traverse your right to exist, to have an opinion... wanting to be validated and appreciated simply for being you.

If so, I get it because that's exactly how I felt for most of my life. Changing old beliefs and patterns is not easy, especially when those internal voices are complicated by other people that influenced your life along the way and made you feel invisible, too. But the good news is that with some time and intention, change is possible.

Take my mom for instance, who was a beautiful, independent, working woman of her time and came from a large, loving, and supportive family. She had her own job, made her own money, and had created her own life when this suave, red-headed stranger (my father) swept her off her feet.

To my father, this was a woman that in his past, would have been out of his reach. She was a stunning beauty - tall and slim with bright blue eyes and flawless skin. She had a smile and stature that would light up any room. She came from a good, hardworking family that he had always longed for. This was not only a woman that would look good on his arm, but a woman of great elegance and education that could fill the negative spaces he held within from his earlier years.

The marriage happened fairly quickly, as it often did back in those days. And only then did a new (hidden) story begin to emerge about the truth of these two lovebirds.

With their union, my mother moved away from her parents and six sisters for the very first time. She followed my dad throughout his stint in the military, going from post to post in different cities, and soon began to experience the two sides to my father. On one hand he was fun, charming, and magnetic (the person she had fallen in love with) who could be the life of the party. And on the other hand, he was aggressive, overly-driven, and controlling, a side that was hard to hide (and hard to endure).

As the controlling side of my dad became more and more apparent, it became more difficult for my mom to cope. She had always been smart and a bright light, but there had also always been a hint of shyness that surrounded her. In his presence, with the absence of her family, her light began to dim, and the more time that passed, the more alone she felt. This loneliness sent her inward, taking solace in bottles of vodka. My mother began secretly drinking by herself, filling Coca-Cola bottles with liquor to numb and soothe the emptiness.

The lack of immediate family nearby paired with the responsibility of raising two children (at the time), and dealing with the controlling part of my father took a major toll on her spirit.

My mother continued to drink throughout the years, trying to cover up her tears as she was moved further away from her own family. When I came into the picture (the 3rd child and the youngest of the family), I often wondered why it felt so hard to feel close to my mother. I wondered why she didn't want to do things with me, or be part of the mother-daughter events that often took place where we lived. This left a huge imprint on the little girl within me, which left me feeling like I didn't matter and like maybe, there really was something wrong with me. As an innocent young girl, I didn't understand alcoholism. All I knew (or what I believed) was that my mom didn't want me around. When really, she was preoccupied with her own inner demons, doing whatever she could to keep any semblance of normalcy in the household.

LONGING FOR LOVE

I longed for a father and mother who saw me, who encouraged me, who made me feel loved, who would teach me to navigate through the emotional highs and lows of childhood. I wanted parents that were supportive, and excited about showing me what a loving relationship looked and felt like. I didn't want a life of fake fairytale endings that I read in books. I wanted *real!* Maybe you can relate.

Instead, I got absent parents who when they were around, were too busy to notice me. I felt less than worthy, ignored and unloved. And when you feel invisible and unwanted, it's easy to be triggered when someone ignores you. Even the smallest things can cause flashbacks of the past to pop up, turning your current reality upside down.

It can also be very normal for people that grow up with these kinds of beliefs to wonder if they can really make a difference in the world, or believe that because they never felt important to their caregivers, they must be insignificant in the world. But I promise you this - you are worthy and enough and you belong. You are important, and significant, no matter where you came from.

I had a longing to be praised and encouraged... to be seen! But instead, I felt alone and invisible, and because of this, I struggled to really understand myself and who I was. For decades, I was so worried about what others wanted and needed that I failed to look at what it was that I wanted and needed.

My upbringing, and the lack of love I felt shaped me tremendously. There was a lack of understanding as to what the rules and expectations were at home. My mom's drastic changes from no rules to strict disciplinary action was confusing. My father would try to enforce whatever rules were in place when he was home, but even that felt strange, which left me to my own devices, making up my own set of rules to live by.

I was a smart kid and like many that are too smart for their own good, I became a master at manipulating the rules to make my parents happy and still get what I wanted. Turns out this was good for me in the short-term, but bad in the long-run. I never learned structure, or discipline, so coping as an adult became very difficult to maneuver as I grew up.

A child is supposed to push the boundaries, that's a given. They have not matured enough to understand the consequences, which is where parents come into play. When children live in a state of confusion, and a home that does not have any basic structure, or a sense of order, they may begin to feel like they do not belong. Or like me, like they just don't matter. It's the job of the parent to push back with love, not neglect.

BECOMING

I did not know who I was without the opinions or demands of others. I learned to pretend and became a master chameleon, changing my colors with every person I met. I just wanted to fit in. No matter what I did, or who I became in the process, my internal confidence continued to waiver. I got really good at being an imposter to appease others which may sound great - but it was crushing me inside.

I spoke briefly of my sister in the first chapter, and how she was my angel. In so many ways, she was the complete opposite of me. She had jet black hair, brown eyes and olive skin (from our Native Indian heritage), which was a total contrast to my fair skin, blue eyes and blonde locks. I tended to be more gregarious, to her shy personality and introspective demeanor. Yet if put side by side, there was no mistake that we were sisters.

She was an old soul, who unfortunately, lived a short life. But while she was here, she was able to instill her deep wisdom in me during those secret poker games, and smoke ring lessons. Her words were always so powerful and to this day, continue to live within me. I would grab onto the hope she instilled in me each time I would make a bad decision, praying there was enough rope to keep me afloat, and bring me back to life.

I became dependent on my sister's love and support, and over the years, our bond continued to grow. Like the time my dad made the decision to send my mom, sister and myself to travel through Asia for 3 weeks. I was 19 (Ginger was 29) and we were supposed to keep an eye on my Mom, who had had a mental breakdown because of the drinking. My father believed this trip would be good for her while she was recovering.

But one night, after my mom had fallen asleep, my sister and I snuck away for a couple hours to the rooftop bar in the hotel where we were staying in Tokyo Japan. We wanted to relax and be able to talk freely as sisters, without the responsibility of babysitting our mother.

Ginger had ordered a Top of Tokyo Martini, and I ordered a drink called, Sex on The Beach (this was a treat as I would have been underage back home). We sat alone chatting, laughing and discussing our trip while enjoying the rooftop view and specialty drinks when Ginger casually turned toward me...

"I love you, Pod," which was her special nickname for me. "I have something to tell you... I'm gay." I remember looking at her with a straight face and reassuring her that it didn't matter, I loved her no matter what. To which I then confessed, "I date black guys!" Which made us laugh because both of those topics were considered taboo to talk about (and live) back in the early 70's. But between us, there was no judgement, just the unconditional love we had for each other as sisters, and best friends.

We don't all have a bright light in our life like I had with my sister. In such cases, we have to learn how to become our own light in the darkness. Ginger helped me hang on, there's no doubt about that! But I still had to learn to grab onto life's setbacks, and pull myself up. A lesson I wish I'd understood much earlier.

THE BUTTERFLY EMERGES

If you grew up in a home without any sense of control, or healthy boundaries, clear expectations, or structure, then it's likely you struggle finding your own compass to guide your decisions. All of this can contribute to feeling unseen, unheard, even unloved.

If you've ever questioned your behaviors, or felt invisible, longing for someone to really SEE you and understand you, this is an invitation to take any of the unresolved anger, frustration, or pain you have been holding onto and use it to move you forward. Not with bitterness or resentment, but with love and compassion, allowing these emotions to push you towards recovery and change, which will allow your soul to sing.

Sure, you have scars, and possibly even some open wounds. We all do to some degree. But you must be willing to acknowledge your inner self and look within to see and feel the hurt of your confused inner child in order to create a new story from it all. By doing so, you will get to know her on a deeper level while showing her that there is a connection between who you were and who you are becoming. And to know that there is a world filled with love out there... even if this is the first time she's witnessed it.

Commit to being there for that little girl who has been masquerading as an adult all these years feeling unwanted, invisible, and constantly seeking validation. Any unintentional self-sabotage can be released - and your story can be rewritten. Regardless of your past, you can live the life you've always dreamed of and you are deserving of it all.

Once you are willing to see and acknowledge your inner little girl, it becomes much easier to commit to being there for her. Turn toward the pain, and let your little girl within be felt by you. When you begin to recognize the record playing in your head, and embrace your weaknesses and poor choices, you will begin the process of self-acceptance, and the healing can finally begin.

Think back through your own story, as I have no doubt that you too, have people in your life that stood out. Maybe you had an angel (like I did with my sister) that built you up and inspired you... Someone you looked up to - a friend, a teacher, a grandmother - that saw your spark within, and encouraged you to dream big, and to shoot for the stars.

Or maybe there was a stranger who saw your light and was gracious and kind to you, and reminded you that you mattered (such as, "You have the prettiest lashes."). We all have someone that believes in our dream to travel over the rainbow and sees our light within. I promise you, it's still there. The light may have dimmed, but it's not gone.

The smallest act, or the simplest words can sometimes make a big difference as to which path you take, especially when you are at a crossroads. You may not have recognized them as such at the time, but isn't it funny how positive words and experiences inevitably find their way back into our minds when we need them most? Maybe it's as we are about to make a critical life decision, or possibly in the face of something that feels really challenging.

These are the exact acts and words we should be holding onto and remembering. Not the negative words of the bully, or the relative that said something hurtful. Because like all of us, they have their own story and chances are good that their ugliness has nothing to do with you.

Children need consistency and limits, they need basic discipline, and they need to know and understand that someone is in charge. But it needs to be mixed in with love, compassion, and motivation. Intuitively, kids know there are unspoken rules. And I believe they also realize (at some point, anyway) that discipline is good for them. But it is their job *as children* to push the limits - and it's the parent's job to hold strong and retain order and structure to help raise healthy adults instead of damaged, grown, adult-like people.

Like me, you may not have received this support and consistency as a child. But as an adult, you can change all of that, and break the cycle.

It's okay to be scared. You can do it. There are always bright lights in our lives, whether we see them or not. And sometimes we need to look harder to find the light so we can turn it on, or grab the rope a little harder to help ourselves up. Either way, that little girl inside is ready to heal (or you wouldn't be reading this book). Your time is now, and you don't have to do any of it alone.

REFLECTION

Who in your life has positively shaped and/or inspired you (beliefs, opinions, etc.)? Have you expressed your gratitude for their role in your life? If not, take this time to do that now.

3

HOLLOW EYES, EMPTY SOUL

Her sad eyes
sung stories
with sad endings,
I wanted to wrap her in a blanket
and tell her she would be safe forever,
and so I did.

- Atticus

I was about 8 when my parents decided to move to Marymoor Farm in Redmond, WA. It was finally move-in day, and my dad piled us all into his big 1960 yellow Lincoln Continental. Heading down the road, I could feel the excitement permeate through my body. That, of course mixed with anxiousness and even some reluctance about the move, as I thought about all the unknowns that lie ahead.

We drove for what seemed like hours, as my stomach twisted and turned with anticipation. Then finally, the car began to slow, and my dad turned into a long, tree-lined driveway. I quickly rolled the car window down to feel the fresh air on my face, and get a better look of my new home. It was a warm, sunny day, and aside from the small breeze I could feel against my face, the only other sound I could hear was that of the tires clickety-clacking over an old wooden bridge.

As I looked up from the ground, my curious eyes became wide. In front of me was the biggest, most beautiful house I could have ever imagined. "Is that our house?" I loudly asked my father. And with a big smile, he replied that yes, it sure was.

I could not believe it, it was magical, and looked like a castle right out of a storybook. The grass was so green and beautiful and the yard was so big! I couldn't wait to do cartwheels for miles and miles with my sister. The trees were so tall, they must have touched the sky, and I felt giddy at the thought of climbing them. And there was a swing! A big tire swing hanging from the largest and strongest tree in the whole wide world. I was so incredibly happy that the wait to explore and see what adventures lie ahead felt almost unbearable.

When my dad finally stopped the car, I immediately jumped out, running as fast as I could up the walkway to the magical front door of our real life castle! I waited impatiently for the others, hardly being able to contain myself. As my dad approached the front door and slowly took out the key, he smiled as he teased me, taking his time just to hear my squeal. As the door flung open he yelled to us kids, "now go find your bedroom." I remember giving him an awkward surprise hug thinking, *could this actually be happening? Is this really our home? Did I really get to have my very own room in a castle?* I felt like Cinderella! Well, after she'd escaped her evil step-family, that is.

I ran into the house and up the stairs, and into the first bedroom I saw. To the right of the door, just as you walked in, was an exquisite set of built-in white shelves that ran about 5 feet long, with an abundance of drawers in different sizes, which created a perfect spot to display all my toy horses, as well as a place to keep my secret treasures I'd collected. My single bed would fit perfectly right around the corner up against the shelves, along with all my stuffed animals and my school desk. The room was full of natural light with windows all around. I just knew this was the perfect room for me. I had my very own bedroom, which immediately became my special sanctuary.

The whole house, which was built in the early 1900's, was captivating. With its secret drawers and hallways, and the vast acres of woods and fields to play in, I felt like the luckiest girl alive to get to call this magical place my home.

This new home would be full of never-ending adventures and exploration, where my curiosity would keep me entertained for hours on end. I felt like there was no way I would ever feel alone here, which made me excited to express my creative mind freely. Our new castle offered me countless hours of play, joy, and escapism. It fit right in line with the life I had learned to live, not knowing or understanding how it would affect me in the future.

MAGIC THROUGH A CHILD'S EYES

Over the next few days and weeks, I explored the acres of property. There were horses, cows, pigs, and chickens, all of which were cared for by the many farm hands, and groundskeepers that lived onsite. I loved all the animals, especially the horses and cows. I would talk to them daily, and eventually I was allowed to help bring in the dairy cows at night to milk them, along with learning to ride the horses.

Most of the farm hands were older than myself, and I eventually became affectionately known as "the girl in the big house." I believed I was living the ultimate little girls dream, gone for hours, lost every day in my own imagination, focused on all the possibilities and travels that I believed lay just around the next corner.

I became fast friends with a girl my age that lived on the farm named Karen. We did everything together. We would go on our daily farm adventures, like building the biggest hay forts with secret passageways in the red barn on the back 40 of the farm where no one could find us. As well as selling lost golf balls from the creek that ran through our property back to the golfers for a penny. When Karen couldn't come out and play, I would be happy and content riding the horses or playing in my room with all my imaginary friends. My little life felt like such a dream, one that I didn't want to wake up from.

When the nights were warm, I would go outside, and lay on the soft, inviting lawn while looking up at the millions of twinkling stars. I always found myself searching the sky for shooting stars and imagining a world where I could travel over the rainbow, where there would be no problems, only love, laughter and happiness. I would bring my cat, Gina and all the animals of the world to a safe place

25

where they could run freely and be happy. Those nights, looking up at the stars, always made me feel special, like I was someone who belonged. I felt like the stars were winking at me and telling me softly, "you matter" which is all I really wanted.

DIFFERENT INSIDE

Even though Marymoor was one of the happiest places in my life, I always felt different from other kids my age. I felt like an outcast, lost and empty, constantly wondering if I would ever fit in or find someone that could love somebody that was different on the inside like I was.

I would see other parents and how they seemed to act towards their children, so loving and caring, giving them hugs and soft kisses on the forehead. I longed to feel loved and cared for in this way. Whenever I saw this, there would be a pang of sadness that washed over me, along with a deep rooted belief that I was unlovable and unworthy of the same kind of love my friends received from their parents. I didn't know why, exactly. But it felt true.

At times I would cry quietly in my bed while holding onto one of my dolls or my cat who would snuggle up against me. But as I got older, things changed and instead of crying, I would shrug my shoulders, put on my happy face and give my pets a big hug telling them, "we will be alright." Animals were always a source of the love I was seeking, and made me feel cared for and understood. I had yet to find another human who I felt really understood me, aside from my sister, but she was older, and she had her own life to tend to.

This was my happy place, and I never wanted to leave.

I'd like you to take a moment and close your eyes. Take a deep breath and think about your own happy place as a kid. Was it by the sea with the sounds of the ocean and the feeling of the salt water running over your feet on a warm day? Or maybe in the mountains where the air was fresh and clean, and you could hear a waterfall off into the distance. Or maybe it was when you were riding your brand new red bike with the silver spokes and ribbons from the handlebars that flew back with the wind.

Think about how your happy place made you feel. For me, my happy place brought about a sense of freedom, exhilaration, childlike wonder, and awe. I remember being in that place and wishing the moment would last forever.

Now think about your life today. Where is your happy place now? And what are the feelings you experience when you're there, fully embodied in the beauty of it all?

As adults, we often fail to allow ourselves to truly be in the experience of pure joy. We become so focused on the adult-stuff (like, responsibilities) that we forget what it feels like to really be happy and joyful. But what I've found to be incredibly powerful is to remember what happiness felt like as a child, and then allow myself to do whatever I need to do to find that same level of ecstacy in my day to day life as an adult.

Having this "place" to focus on, or maybe even go to, can be so therapeutic, especially in moments of overwhelm. I've also found it to be a powerful practice in the moments that we find ourselves seeking love outside of ourselves, forgetting that the love we are looking for is and has always been within us. If you were like me as a child, and felt like a total outcast, having your "escape" was probably not only helpful, but necessary. But I want you to remember something…

Your happy place can be created at any moment because just like the love that we all desire to feel, your happy place is also within you.

Your true self, your "home," your soul, and the very place you desire to have filled up, it's all here. All you have to do is open yourself up to receiving the gifts available, and releasing any doubt or external influences blocking your truth.

It takes work. It takes time. It takes courage and bravery and honesty. But with all of that comes a sense of freedom that can only be felt, not explained in words. And to me, that's worth all the discomfort for I know that with that also comes immense amounts of happiness.

THE PIVOTAL PORTRAIT

As a child growing up, I was cared for but not nurtured. I felt powerless, voiceless, and unimportant. By keeping my feelings and thoughts to myself, this put me in self-preservation mode, and became the only way I knew to really feel safe. As a child (and really, as an adult, too) you learn who you are and how to be based on your real-life circumstances. As such, the ability to emotionally or intellectually understand what is different about you and why can be confusing, frustrating and shameful.

My differences were confirmed when at age of 10, my mother called me downstairs and said she had commissioned a well-known painter to paint my portrait. Now, I did not really understand why, or what this meant, but that one experience alone would be pivotal, and haunt me for the next 45 years.

That following Monday was the day that Harold was to arrive and begin painting my portrait. My mom told me to go up to my room, and put on my prettiest dress. I felt cheerful that day and chose my favorite outfit, which was a black velvet jumper with pink and white flowers on the suspenders and a white blouse with ruffles around the collar. And of course my shiny black patent-leather Mary Jane shoes with white ribbon socks. I felt good and thought I looked beautiful. I remember being in high spirits with great anticipation for the day.

When Harold arrived, my mom introduced me to him as he set up his easel on the front porch, closest to the pool area. He seemed old and had a ratty looking beard and a faint, yet familiar smell of alcohol wafting from his breath. I knew that smell from the parties my parents would throw where they thought it was cute to have me serve drinks to their friends. In that moment, my high spirits dropped and all of a sudden, I felt like this might not be as fun as I had initially anticipated.

Our front porch was one of my favorite places. You could see the trees, my beloved swing, and the big green lawn where I would practice my cartwheels and somersaults daily. But today, instead of going out to play in the yard, I had to sit still in an uncomfortable chair while this funny smelling man painted my portrait for hours, which for a kid, felt like eternity.

Harold came back every day for the next 5 days to paint me. I thought I was doing very well, sitting still and being quiet in that chair when really, all I wanted to do was go play. Until the 6th and final day when Harold didn't show up. I actually didn't care as I was happy to run off and do kid things, but my mom was not happy. Not in the least.

After weeks of calls, frustration and excuses, my parents were finally able to speak with Harold. He told them that he would not be returning to finish my portrait because I was "too fidgety" and because of my "sad, empty and soulless eyes." I had no idea what that even meant, but in my mind it was just further validation of my unworthiness.

I never saw Harold again.

That unfinished portrait was left to look back at me for years. There were no flowers on my suspenders, which was my favorite part of my outfit, and all I could see were my hollow eyes he'd painted on my fair-skinned face staring straight into my own, wondering why I looked so sad in the first place?

I felt ashamed and upset, and like once again, this was somehow all my fault. My parents paid good money to hire an acclaimed artist to paint my portrait and because of my "sad, empty, soulless eyes," he refused to come back and finish the project. Nothing was ever said, but I believed in my little girl mind that I was a disappointment to my mom and dad. This was just one of the many experiences of my young life that left me feeling even more alienated and misunderstood.

The truth was, the artist had managed to capture the real me that I had been unwilling to see, or maybe just unwilling to admit. I had believed in my mind that I was doing a great job at hiding and only showing the world what I thought they wanted to see - happiness and beauty. But as it turned out, I was projecting emptiness and detachment, which were in fact, my internal truth.

This unfinished portrait hung in my home for a long time. And each time I would see it, I was reminded of the little girl longing for love, and seeking it in all the wrong places. I was reminded that I was sad, empty, and soulless and now I had a picture to prove it.

REFLECTION

Where do you go to find your happy place? Carve out time in your calendar in the next week to spend time there. Then write down how it makes you feel. You're worth it!

4

DADDY, WHY DON'T YOU
LOVE ME?

The depth
of your love
will forever show
in your daughter's eyes.

- Michelle W. Emerson

very afternoon, about 30 minutes before the school bell rang,
I would get this anxious feeling in my belly as I was preparing
my escape from the drudgery of the school day. I often found
myself daydreaming about traveling to new lands rather than listening
to history lessons (or anything else, really). I found everything about
school boring, and admittedly, only did what was necessary to get by
with a passing grade. I always tried to slide into a seat in the back of
the room in hopes that my teachers wouldn't call on me because when
I was caught off guard, my slight stutter would come out, which made
me want to slump down in my chair and disappear.

Every day was the same thing... watch the clock as the school
day came to an end so that as soon as the bell rang, I could get the
hell out of that place! Without fail, I was always the first one out the
door with my books in hand, rushing to be anywhere but school.

The hallways were always bustling with students, all headed out the doors in different directions. Being my clever self, I'd found a way to meander through the crowds, and rush out through a lesser known side door which led to the back corner of the baseball field where I would meet up with my besties, Cathy and Marlene.

The three of us became fast friends and for a few years, we did everything together. We were all a bit different (misfits), none of us feeling like we quite fit in with the rest of the girls in school. Our differences created a bond of sisterhood that no one could break.

Every day after school, the three of us would make the long walk back towards our homes through the woods with our books in hand. We would chat about how silly boys were, laugh like crazy, and solidify plans as to whose house we would be spending the weekend at, which was usually Cathy's because she had the best backyard. Plus, her parents were always so happy to see us. They also let us sleep outside in a tent when the weather was good and they always barbequed the best hamburgers for us. I felt so welcomed at their house, like a part of their family. Something I'd longed to feel in my own home.

Each day, at the same corner we would part ways, as I would turn towards my house and Cathy and Marlene would continue on down the long hill towards their homes. I would smile, wave and say, "see you tomorrow morning!" before walking the remaining 2 blocks to my house and up the long driveway as I called for my cat, Gina, a small 3-year old tabby who brought me so much joy. She would greet me every day in the driveway with a big stretch, and I would pick her up and give her a big hug as we entered our quiet and empty house together.

As I walked through the tall wooden front doors, holding Gina under my arm, I'd head straight down the hall to my bedroom, giving Gina a gentle squeeze and placing her on my bed where she would dig deep under the covers and curl up and take a cat nap. She loved a nice warm spot in the bed after a long day of exploration outside. Pulling off my jacket, I'd then line up my school books on my small desk in proper order in preparation for doing my homework for the evening.

Before getting started on my studies, I'd head into the kitchen to make my favorite afternoon snack - a bologna, mayonnaise and pickle sandwich! Our large kitchen overlooked the front yard and I could see the other kids playing across the way. They always looked so happy and I often found myself making up stories about how much their parents loved them, and probably showed them with hugs and praise, while wishing I could experience that same kind of love from my own parents. I'd then pour myself a glass of milk, pick up my sandwich and venture back into my room to eat and start my homework. I always made it a point to finish my homework before my parents got home from work, as I grew to realize how important that simple task was in order to keep the peace.

I loved this time all to myself. It was quiet and the silence gave me space to sit alone and daydream about all the travels I would take in the future, the house that I would buy someday, and the wonderful life I would eventually live. These were my two hours of pure freedom before my mom would get off work and arrive home to begin fixing dinner and I soaked up every minute.

On the days where I would finish my homework early, I would often go downstairs into my dad's office and sit in his big soft leather swivel chair, and spin it around. I always seemed to find something new, like a photograph with my father looking dapper in a custom suit and tie sitting or standing next to a famous person, such as Jack Dempsey (the famous boxer) or a high profile CEO.

I'd look around and see if there were any new sales awards on the wall, which there always seemed to be. They'd say things like, "Top Sales Person, Jack M. Love" or "Top Producer of The Year, Jack M. Love."

All these plaques and pictures made me so proud of my father. I wanted so badly to be just like him someday. I would imagine my own name on one of those plaques, so I could show him that his little girl was deserving of his love. I thought that if I became just like him then he would be proud of me, and love me the same way I loved him.

PERSISTENCE CHANGES EVERYTHING

My dad always seemed to be reading different articles. He had shelves of books in his office, along with journals, and notebooks that were neatly arranged on the shelves along his walls. While in my dad's office perusing one day, I noticed a book lying face down on his desk that intrigued me. I picked it up, noting the page it was on so I could place the book back exactly the way I'd found it. The book was called, "Think and Grow Rich" by Napoleon Hill. As I picked it up, I noticed the chapter name, PERSISTENCE, and began to turn one page, then another. I was instantly fascinated with the ideas interwoven throughout the pages about getting everything you wanted in life if you were just *persistent*. Which sparked a thought: *THIS is how I can win my dad's love! I can learn everything I need to know to be successful and if I'm persistent, I'll eventually become just like him, and then he will love me, and everything will be perfect.*

I thought that *becoming like him* would be the best way for my father to acknowledge me. I would learn to speak his sales language and negotiate with him. I was sure this was the missing link I had been searching for.

Unlike school, this interested me, and I was a quick study when it came to the words in these books. Day after day, I would sneak downstairs to read my dad's books, especially when he was out of town. I ferociously read every book I could get my hands on with titles such as, The Art of Public Speaking and How To Win Friends and Influence People.

And so it began. Without really meaning to (not consciously, anyway), I learned to become someone else when speaking to my dad. I began negotiating my allowance, chores, and even persuaded him to let me go out with my friends. He seemed to find this entertaining and fun, and it became a game between us. This was our special bond that none of my other siblings had with him which finally made me feel special. I was becoming his little salesperson, which seemed to make him happy. But in reality, I was losing myself in the process, becoming an imposter in my own life. Because of this, as the years went by I no longer recognized the real me any longer. As a matter of fact, I'm not sure I actually knew who I was in the first place. Sure, I was a kid, but I'd gotten so good at becoming what I thought my father wanted that subconsciously I began to put any semblance of my truth aside, buying into my own BS in the process.

I had become his little salesperson on the surface, a pretty little girl that he showed off and encouraged to pretend to play the organ to impress his friends or act like a bartender at the cocktail parties he would host. I was becoming a great show person, just like my father - at the expense of myself.

I could turn on the charm, and the smiles instantly to get his attention. I did exactly what he wanted (and had come to expect) and in return, I would receive what I mistakenly believed I wanted - the money, cars, and clothes - all of which left me in a constant state of loneliness with a gaping hole in my heart. I didn't understand why I felt this way. While this was not the type of love I wanted, it was something! So why did I still have these feelings of emptiness? The line was getting more and more confusing between what I thought real love should look and feel like, and the love I was actually receiving from my father.

COPING THROUGH CONFUSION

None of it made any sense to me, and I didn't know how to cope with the confusion. As I headed into my late teens, the hole in my heart only got bigger, and my coping skills, for lack of a better term, sucked. By my early twenties, I was making bad decisions and running with the wrong crowd. Add to that my inability to choose "good" men. Instead, being drawn to those that were emotionally unavailable, dating them and believing that they cared about me only to realize that no, they didn't. Because they couldn't! It was like a broken record with each one and as I allowed myself to open up a bit more to let each of them in, I found myself being used and abused, over and over again.

I dove into drugs as a way to escape my reality, which only made me feel even more worthless. I believed that I would never be good enough for my father, or anyone. I kept all of this inside because I learned early on not to show my vulnerabilities, as I believed they were signs of weakness. The confusion I felt paired with the unconscious transformation of myself to become who I thought my father wanted me to be not only led me to feel utterly empty and lost, but it had me headed in a deadly direction.

It wasn't until later in life that I understood the quiet love my father showed me was love, it was just different from what I thought it "should" look like. He didn't nurture me because he wasn't nurtured by his parents. But he loved me in his own way, and that was by putting a beautiful roof over my head, showing me the pleasures of expensive restaurants, and never wanting for anything. He showed his love by giving me things that he never had and that was his strength, not the hugs or the I love you's. He gave his love through unexpected surprises like a trip to Hawaii for the family or the weekend he spent building a warm, safe place for my cat, Gina to sleep outside. He knew I loved animals, but because he didn't know how to express himself verbally, he did it through acts of kindness and gifts. I only wish I would have understood all this when I was younger, before his early death.

My dad was a man of great strength and perseverance. He showed me his love in ways that were foreign to me, but that doesn't mean they weren't valid and kind. I will always be grateful for the way he loved me, and the lessons he taught me about work ethic, charisma, and striving to be my best. And while there was always a light burning deep inside of me, my father didn't know how to turn that switch on. I now know it's not because he didn't want to, but because he didn't know any better.

The bond we had, although unconventional, will always be special in my heart, which is exactly where my dad is today. There were so many things I wish I had known, as my future self would have responded differently. But life has a funny way of throwing us curve balls, and it is how we choose to respond when we miss that ball that teaches us strength, courage and forgiveness so that we can find our own way and persevere no matter the circumstances.

Daddy, if you're listening, I love you. I always have, and I always will.

REFLECTION

Have you received mixed signals in your life that put you in a state of confusion, and made you feel powerless? How did you pivot to create better feelings within?

5

BECOMING WHAT THEY WANTED

I feel stuck right in the middle
of guilt and circumstances
part shame and part blame
the ultimate self-sabotage

where the montage of my life
and the mirage of my future
are caught in between
a moment of truth;

all I can remember
on one hand is inside,
a barrage of my past faults
leading the entourage of my future

and on the other, outside,
a collage of sticky conditions
which made me act out of character
I was helpless, had no one for succor

so here I am
caught in between then and hereafter
trapped in my own espionage
my camouflaged authenticity, unmasked

I feel stuck right in the middle
of guilt and circumstances
my corsage of now
dislodged, self-sabotaged

- T. Kagalwalla.

After spending years being (unconsciously) groomed by my father to be the best salesperson I could be, I learned the art of becoming what everyone else wanted me to be. In many ways, this skillset served me well and really helped me to fit in and garner opportunities that may have otherwise gone to someone else. But on the other hand, because of my deep seated need to be loved and my ability to conform to others desires, I had no idea who I was or what I wanted, making it really hard to set and reach my own goals in order to make *myself* proud - and genuinely feel happy and fulfilled.

It wasn't until I jumped into new territory and applied for a job (that I didn't even know I wanted) that I was able to see just how far removed I had become from my truth. That one decision, although it didn't play out in the way I'd envisioned, lit a fire in my belly that gave me hope for my future. And ultimately, allowed me to prove to myself that I could do anything I put my mind to and I didn't actually need the approval of anyone to follow my own bliss.

WELCOME TO THE FRIENDLY SKIES

I could not have been more over the moon excited then when I was chosen over hundreds and hundreds of other applicants to become one of five flight attendants hired by Northwest Orient Airlines out of Seattle in 1973.

It all began when my best friend, Sue from high school called to tell me that she saw the perfect job opportunity for me in the paper. "You should be a flight attendant! You would be perfect with your infectious smile and positive attitude; people would love you!

They're interviewing at the Seattle airport this weekend. You need to go try out!"

She was right to reach out. I definitely felt I needed something more solid at this point in my life. Although I'd always felt a bit lost, the truth of the matter was I was growing up, and it was time to root myself into something with meaning. Something that brought me joy and gave me purpose.

Sue always seemed to know what I needed before I did. She was attuned on a deep level, which made our friendship that much more special. We had many conversations throughout our teenage years, and into our young adult years as well, about her family and mine. Her family was overly strict while my mom, who drank a lot, was not strict at all, and the dynamic between my father and I (when he was home) was complicated at best.

We were on the opposite ends of the spectrum as far as our home life was concerned, but as friends, we had a close connection that I valued deeply. Sue always seemed to have a sense of innate wisdom about her which is why I believe she saw something in me that I didn't. She saw the *real* me, the one that struggled with who I was at my core, yet persisted nonetheless with strength, determination and courage.

She could see my insecurities, even through the smiles, and my need to break free from the control aspects of my father. She believed in me and that meant everything! When she mentioned the opportunity with the airlines, I decided it was time to step out of the comfort I'd created with my family and take a chance on myself and my happiness for the first time. I needed to break the chains, and I wanted to. I finally felt like I was ready, or as ready as I'd ever be! Little did I know, though, that those chains would be much harder to break than I'd anticipated.

This would be the first time I had done something on my own without my father's guidance or financial assistance. Prior to this, I was forced into opportunities (that I was not at all excited about). Or told that I should work with my father in his leasing office in order to have an income of my own. I had flunked out of college, after all, with no other promising job possibilities in front of me. Because of that, I worked under the constraints of my fathers' thumb for years. That is, until Sue called to tell me about a potentially life-changing opportunity to fly the friendly skies.

CALL TO COURAGE

I felt so proud, like I was finally going to be a "somebody." At the time, it was considered "elite" for a woman to become a flight attendant and I saw this as a badge of honor of sorts with an opportunity to travel and explore the world, something I had dreamt of since I was a little girl. And this time, I was doing it all on my own.

Sue was totally right, which seemed to be pretty typical when it came to understanding me better than even I could at the time. This opportunity really was the perfect fit for me, and there was no way I would let the hundreds of other beautiful, intelligent applicants that were in line intimidate me. I was determined to get this job, whatever it took. So I did what I did best - I turned on the smiles, the charisma, and all I had learned from the books I'd read and the dance I'd mastered between me and my father. I knew exactly what to say, and when to say it, and although there was a nagging voice in my head questioning the authenticity of my actions, the imposter within was born for this role (and humbly, I was brilliant at it). Whether it was the real me or not, I felt empowered and free. And I loved it!

There were multiple interviews to go through and to my surprise, I kept being called back! I was a nervous wreck, but felt confident that this was the right decision for me, and the answer to all my prayers. They continued to whittle down the list of applicants, and moved us into smaller rooms until there were only 20 of us left. They ran us through one-on-one life scenarios where afterwards we'd get a "thank you," or be moved to the next designated room to wait.

I was surprised at my ability to remain calm on the outside while inside, my blood was racing through my veins at 100 miles an hour. I did not even realize how much I wanted this job until there were only ten of us left, and I knew they were only hiring five.

As we waited patiently in the musty room, they called us in one at a time. We all stood together in silence, looking at each other with obvious anticipation and nerves. It was so quiet you could hear a pin drop! We all knew that five applicants would be going home by the end of the day and one by one, individuals were called into the room, never to be seen again.

After about half an hour of complete silence between the final applicants, there were three of us left when a very pretty, well-groomed lady opened the door and called my name, "Patricia Love, please follow me."

As I anxiously walked through the door and down the hall into a separate room, I noticed one man and two women who appeared to be in their late 30's sitting next to each other on the couch with their hands folded in their laps. They all looked very stoic and I felt like I had just been called into the principal's office.

One of the ladies smiled and asked me to sit in the chair. I was now feeling sick to my stomach, and I must have looked like a deer in headlights! She introduced herself as Sylvia and said she managed all the flight attendants for Northwest Orient. She then turned to the others and introduced them as her assistants before pausing for a moment as she looked at the other two people sitting on the couch. All I could think was, *this isn't good, I'm definitely going home...* and I wanted to puke.

And then I saw a big grin spread across Sylvia's face, "Welcome to Northwest Orient!" I was speechless! I heard her talking, and saying something about training in Minneapolis, which would start in just a few weeks, but I couldn't seem to wrap my head around what had just happened.

I sat there for what seemed like forever before I was able to get my wits about me and was able to speak. "I am so excited for this opportunity. Thank you! I can fly back anytime you need me."

Life as I knew it had just changed in an instant. I was in shock! I heard them say a few more things, before giving me some paperwork to take with me. They said they would be in touch to coordinate all the travel arrangements then asked me to leave through the other door (not the door I came in, which I guess is why we never saw anyone come back out). I nodded my head and stood up, turning directly to all of them, and with a big smile, I thanked them once again for this wonderful opportunity. I calmly turned and went out the door, but my insides were doing flips from the excitement.

I did it! I made this happen, all on my own. I had made it through two days of rigorous interviews with <u>600 other applicants</u> - and I'd made it to the final five that were hired. And then it hit me... *I was actually going to be a flight attendant! Holy shit!* I had never tried so hard to succeed at something in my life and here I was, realizing a dream I didn't even know I had when all of this began. I felt like my life was finally going in the right direction and I was being entrusted by complete strangers to make people's travel experiences comfortable, enjoyable, and safe.

I couldn't wipe the smile from my face as I walked to my car. I was tired, yet exhilarated all at the same time. I felt like I was finally *somebody*, and I was proud of myself for the first time that I could ever remember.

FINDING MY WAY

A few weeks later, Northwest sent me to St. Paul, Minneapolis for 8 weeks of intense onsite training and classes. It was the first time that I aced every test taken, both written and oral. I was in my element, and I remembered back to my days as a kid when I would lie on my bed with my cat, listening to music and dreaming of traveling near and far. I remembered being a teenager, lying in my front yard late at night and looking up at the stars, praying for the day that I would be free to explore the world. Even as a kid, I didn't know how I was going to make it happen, but I was determined to figure it out. And here I was, a young adult with my whole life in front of me - and my dreams of traveling over rainbows to faraway places were all coming true.

Unlike my school years growing up, I made friends easily in flight attendant training. After we graduated and became full-time airline employees, a couple of us decided to get an apartment together to share expenses. It was perfect. We all had different schedules so we didn't really see much of each other, and when we did, we spent hours talking about boys, having fun and playing games, like nearly every other young woman in her early 20s. I was pretty, bubbly and full of life, which made me well liked by my peers. And for the first time (maybe ever), I felt genuinely happy and absolutely loved what I was doing.

I thrived with the spontaneity of being on call with only a 2-hour notice, never knowing when or where in the world I might be going, or who I would be flying with. I met all kinds of people and made friends from all over the world. I loved the diversity I was exposed to, and the incredible shopping on layovers was a bonus.

I was never happier than when I was flying, and if I'd had it my way, I would've done it for the rest of my life.

Oddly enough, even though I was living almost 2,000 miles from my father, it was like he still had a hook in me. He never told me I had to do anything, but there was the very real part of me that never wanted to disappoint him. Because of this, I continued to hold the belief that if I did, he wouldn't love me so I made it a point to be conscious of my decisions and how they might affect (my internal story about) his love, and my *worthiness* to be loved by him.

He would ask me to come home for birthdays and holidays. And although I was on probation for the first year with the airlines, as long as I was back for my scheduled flights, traveling in-between wasn't usually a problem. I was constantly jumping on flights back to Seattle to spend time with my idol (my father), and the freedom of being able to do so made me feel on top of the world. But the problem with flying stand-by is that you can't always get a confirmed seat because passengers (understandably) take precedence over employees. Because of this, there was always a possibility of missing a flight, so it was important to plan accordingly.

That first December, after I joined the airlines, my father wanted me to come back to Seattle around Christmas to celebrate my mom. She had worked very hard to give up booze, and had been sober now for about a year. He wanted to do something special for her, and get the whole family together to celebrate. Because of the holiday, there were a lot of people traveling, and even though I was able to get the days off, I was afraid I might be cutting it close if I went home without being able to have a confirmed seat back. This job was everything to me, and I didn't want to jeopardize it.

This particular time, my father was overly persistent. He placed additional guilt on me, and I finally gave in. I said I would come home, but only for 3 days, even though something within me told me it was a mistake.

I flew out on a Thursday evening, and was happy to see my mother looking healthier than she had ever looked. Even my dad seemed to be in rare form, which I'm sure was because he had managed to manipulate our schedules and succeed at getting his entire family back together for Christmas, as my sister and brother also made an appearance, which didn't happen often.

Once again, my father had gotten his way. Our family dynamic was far from conventional, but it's what we knew.

Family dinners had always been very important to my dad. Every Saturday growing up, he would require that everyone in the family be home for Saturday night fondue, where I felt controlled and managed by his expectations. It was always a bit awkward, and a lot of times you could feel the tension in the air along with the relief when it was over.

On this particular trip, I had planned to leave that Saturday evening to be back for work on Monday afternoon… until I was bumped off my flight due to overbooking. Fortunately, I was able to get on another flight the next morning (in the jump seat), and I thought all was going to be fine. Until I got bumped off my connecting flight in Atlanta in order for a paying passenger to get on.

My worst nightmare was coming true.

I was stuck, and although I was constantly calling my supervisors to let them know my circumstances, they were adamant that I needed to figure out a way to get home. I was nervous, and felt extremely anxious as I waited patiently for a seat on any flight I could possibly get on in order to make it home in time for my shift.

But that didn't happen. And I didn't make it back in time.

Devastated, I became silently angry at my father. Or maybe I was mad at myself for caving into his control. I thought that by arranging for someone else to take my shift, given I couldn't seem to get on a flight, I would be in the clear. My shift would be covered, after all. Why would it matter who showed up?

But I was wrong.

SHORT-LIVED DREAMS, LONG-TERM CONSEQUENCES

It had been about 3 weeks since I missed my flight back, and we were now into the New Year. Everything seemed to be going well, and I was happy being back in Minneapolis with the cold, albeit beautiful snow. I had spent New Year's alone with my cat, Pinhead, as Gina had passed away a few years back, and the guy I had recently met and was newly dating was busy with his family.

Just as I'd been growing up, I was more than happy to be on my own. It gave me time to read, clean my house, and watch the mindless TV shows that I loved without interruption.

It was the second Thursday after New Year's and I had a flight scheduled for that afternoon. I was thrilled to have a turnaround flight to LA and back with an 8 hour layover, just enough time to see one of my friends for lunch and a brief catch up.

Just before checking in for my flight, I was called into the office for what I thought was a routine check-in, which often happened to make sure our nails were polished, hair was not too long, and that we hadn't gained weight (yes, they used to weigh us!).

As per usual with these check-ins, I was escorted into the manager's office where I sat down in the chair opposite from him. But this was different. Without hesitation, he looked straight into my eyes and without any expression at all said, "Patricia, we are letting you go. Effective immediately, you are terminated."

I froze, feeling utterly confused. The blood must have drained out of my face too, as I remember feeling extremely weak and lightheaded.

All that I could get out of my mouth was, "why?" I didn't understand how this could be happening. And I didn't think it could have been because I missed my flight 3 weeks ago, as to my understanding, everything was okay since I had gotten someone to take my run.

But he just looked at me with dead eyes, and said, "You are still in the probationary period, and we are letting you go. Pick up your stuff, you are being terminated, and someone else is taking your run today." And that was that. He ordered me out of his office with no real explanation.

Due to my upbringing, I had never been confrontational, so I was scared to say anything. I reluctantly stood up feeling sick and like I could collapse at any moment. I hung my head so my eyes wouldn't meet anyone else's as I rushed through the building and out to my car where I sobbed for an hour before taking the longest drive home of my life.

Within 30 seconds, I went from being a happy, young girl with the whole world ahead of her to feeling completely humiliated. I was not only devastated, but horrified, embarrassed, and sick to my stomach! I thought about what had just happened as my thoughts started down the angry path at my father for making me come home when I knew I shouldn't have. I missed my flight and they fired me for it (or so I thought).

I called my father crying and told him this was all his fault, and he had to fix it! He knew the CEO of Northwest Orient Airlines so he placed a call, hoping to get me my job back. I never knew what was said between them, but apparently there was nothing he could do about it. It was done and just like that, within a matter of minutes, my whole life changed. I had just lost a job that I loved, and I was pissed off at my father for taking away the one thing that made me feel alive and happy!

To make matters worse, I ended up going home early that day only to surprise the guy I was dating by finding him in *my* bed, with my roommate. Apparently he was seeing her behind my back. I had not only just been humiliated by being fired from my job, but I also felt betrayed, mortified and angry at the man I had allowed myself to open up to - someone I trusted with my heart.

This was all too much. Through my seething anger, my eyes saw read and I told them both to get the fuck out of my house.

I stayed in bed for a week, crying, and not speaking to anyone, only getting up to grab more wine and food. I was lost, sick, and didn't want to leave my house or see anybody. I didn't want anyone to know about any of this, either. It was too painful. The job I loved and lost within a year, and the cheating... I didn't have it in me to navigate the emotions I was feeling. Although I didn't care so much about the guy per se, the betrayal cut deep and I just couldn't face the truth of it all, with myself or others. In fact, I was so ashamed that I kept the fact that I'd been fired to myself and lied about why I no longer worked for the airlines for the next 40 years.

That incident was a pivotal point in my life, and took me down a long spiral of blame, shame, self-loathing, and self-sabotaging behavior. I just didn't care anymore, and it was clear that no one really cared about me, either. No one loved me, and by all accounts, my father didn't even seem to care that his selfishness had cost me the one good thing I had in my life. I felt like a total imposter and decided I was going to hide behind my pretty face for the next several years, allowing men to mentally and physically abuse me, getting myself into situations with drugs to escape the pain of being a nobody, and losing myself in the process once again.

RECKLESS AND ALOOF

About 1 month after being let go, I came home from Minnesota and fell further into a depressed state. I didn't want much to do with my parents or family, and to keep to myself, I got a small apartment of my own while working at a little retail shop in the Capital Hill area of Seattle, across the lake about 30 minutes from where I lived.

One night after work, I went to a party on the Seattle side, not far from where I worked. There were a lot of people at the party, playing games and laughing, and I was actually having fun, something I hadn't felt in months! I was relaxed after several drinks, and probably should not have been driving after the party let out, but I did. It was about 1am when I got in my car to head home.

I had only been driving on the freeway for about 10 minutes when I felt a thud, and knew instantly that I had a flat tire. I immediately slowed down to pull the car over and get off the freeway. It was extremely dark, with no freeway lights, and at that time of the night there were almost no cars on the road.

Back then we had no cell phones, just wishful thinking that someone would stop and lend a hand. And thankfully, someone did.

I was so grateful for the kindness of the stranger, a seemingly nice man that took the time to help me out. We chatted while he changed my tire, which took him about a half hour, and when it was fixed, I thanked him, letting him know that I would be forever grateful. But before I could get in my car to leave, his smile turned somber and his eyes became dead as he responded by pulling out a gun, "this is how you're going to repay me."

He told me to turn around as he pushed me hard from behind. I began to plead with him not to hurt me, but it was clear that he had no intention of listening to my pleas nor did he care that I was terrified. He forced me into his car, and raped me that night, all while holding a gun to my head. I was petrified he was going to kill me, so I did what so many people do in the midst of a traumatic experience - I managed to remove myself from my physical body and pretend it wasn't happening.

When he finished, he pushed me out of the car with his foot and left me on the side of the road as if he had just thrown out a piece of garbage, before squealing away with his tires smoking.

I sat for a minute, alone on the side of the freeway, dazed and confused by what had just happened, eventually pulling myself up. I was scared, yet grateful to still be alive.

Somehow I managed to get in my car and drive myself home, where I immediately took a shower. I only told a few people about what had happened that night, and never reported it because I was sure that it was somehow my fault. I had been drinking and I must have done something to make him do this to me (which I now know is completely false). Besides, I had heard that the police would never do anything about it anyway so like everything else, I learned to compartmentalize it, and found a way to move forward, wearing a mask that said, *I'm fine... everything's fine,* just as I had for so many years prior.

This was the true beginning of a long, dark rabbit hole that became (decades of) my life.

YOU CAN RUN, BUT YOU CAN'T HIDE

Within a month I decided to move to California on a whim with my boyfriend at the time. I never let anyone know I was leaving, except my sister, who was the only person I was close to. I gave her my cat, Pinhead to care for, as I didn't know where I might end up. We were both animal lovers, and I knew Pinhead would be safe with her. I also knew that I couldn't stay there any longer... I needed to escape.

My sister and I continued to have a deep bond and she agreed to keep my secret from our parents. However, it didn't take long before my mother found out through a friend that I had left Seattle without a word to anyone. She was appalled and refused to speak to me for months. I personally didn't care though. I didn't care if they loved me or not as I felt they never really loved me anyway. Besides, I believed within my own mind that I didn't deserve love, from them or anyone else so why should it matter that I was, for all intents and purposes, alone.

I was a worthless failure and all I wanted to do was get away from everyone, my life and my father, who I now hated because if it hadn't been for his control, I would still be working for the airlines and none of this would have happened. I was going down a path that would continue to leave me grasping at death's door. And although I knew it, I continued to push the limits, not caring at all about the outcome.

I had been living in Fresno, CA with my boyfriend for about 8 months when one day, as I was out and about, I caught a glimpse of a beautiful silver Rolls Royce sitting in an insurance parking lot out of the corner of my eye. Given the area I was in, this car stood out like a sore thumb and I wondered, *who could the owner be and what did he do to afford such a luxury car?* So I decided to put a note on the windshield asking him to call me because I was interested in learning about how he made his money. It was a rare, bold move on my part, but what did I have to lose? I was already at rock bottom, barely making any money, and stuck in a relationship that had turned abusive.

To my surprise, within a few days the owner of that beautiful Rolls Royce called me. His name was Sal. Sal was a large balding man in his 60's with a cheerful laugh and if it hadn't been for his dark mustache, he could have passed for Santa Claus. He said he was impressed that I had been so forward as to put a note on his car and because of that, he was willing to meet.

For some reason, I found him easy to talk to and told him my story, as well as shared my desire for a chance to make some money and start living a better life. We ended up talking for hours, and he quickly became a good friend and mentor.

He owned Pacific West Insulation, which was a huge company in the Fresno area, and by all accounts, had made Sal a lot of money. I was intrigued.

After spending the next few weeks getting to know each other over daily coffee, he asked if I wanted to sell insulation with his company. He said it would be hard work, but there was a good chance that I could make a great living doing it. My eyes widened and I agreed to give it a go. I was giddy at the new possibility. I mean, why not? At this point, I was willing to do anything to get out of the place I was in, and maybe I would end up with a Rolls Royce, too. How hard could selling insulation be?

Sal gave me his manager's number and after a brief conversation, I was all set to begin the following Monday.

Sal was right. It was hard, and it was tiring, but I was good at it, and I was determined to succeed. It was commission only, but that was okay because the harder I worked, the more money I made. Apparently all my years of reading my dad's books and watching him master his craft was working in my favor. I was the only woman salesperson, which was difficult in the 70's, but I pushed through, ignoring the sexist words and innuendos.

I knew these types of men all too well, and by that time, I wanted no part of it. I kept to myself and showcased a tough exterior, which had become my typical routine. I was doing well selling insulation, and was beginning to find a sense of pride in my work again. But my home life was still a disaster.

After coming home late from a long day at work, I was met by my visibly upset boyfriend who had decided that I must be cheating on him since I'd been gone for so long when in his eyes, I should've already been home. When I tried to explain, he erupted, yelling and screaming, and accusing me of all kinds of things. When I'd previously been directly confronted by men, I would often bow out and leave. But in this situation, I had nowhere to go. He began hitting and kicking me, for what seemed like hours, before raping me and leaving me curled up in a ball in the corner of the house.

When he was finished, I remained still, neither hearing or feeling anything for about an hour before realizing I was truly alone. I slowly picked up my bruised body and drove myself to the emergency room, where they found several broken ribs, along with cuts and bruises all over my body. The nurses were kind, and told me I was lucky, that he could have killed me, and that I should press charges. But I knew I couldn't do that. I just wanted to leave, pretend none of this had ever happened, and be left alone.

Running seemed like the only answer, and had become something I'd gotten used to doing when things got tough, or felt uncomfortable. This was no different.

I knew somewhere in my mind that intellectually, this was wrong, and I didn't deserve this. But emotionally, it was hard to understand. I was scared, embarrassed, and lost (again) and it seemed like no matter what I did to move on and make the most of the situations I had gotten myself into, they haunted me, in one way or another.

I had always been strong, but I knew I couldn't put up with this abuse anymore. Something had to change, and it wasn't going to be him. So I gathered all the strength and courage I could muster and quickly drove back home from the hospital, my body aching and in pain, to do what I had to do.

My boyfriend was still not home so I snuck into the house, keeping all the lights off, and grabbed some clothes and anything of mine that I could fit in my small little red Pinto and left. This time, for good.

I checked into a Motel 6, about 25 miles outside Fresno where no one could find me. I took a well needed shower to wash off the abuse and the rape, and slept for 2 days. When I awoke, I could still feel the physical abuse permeating my entire body and although I was still scared, I felt relieved that I'd made it out alive.

All I kept thinking was, *how the hell did I end up here?* And as I thought about my journey up to this point, I decided to reach for the phone and call my old friend, Sal. I told him what happened, and asked if he could transfer me immediately to his office in San Diego. Without any hesitation, he said yes, and told me to stop by the office before I left to pick up an advance on my commission as he wanted me to have enough money to get to San Diego and find a safe place to stay. He told me that he would call the manager in San Diego, and they would welcome me as soon as I arrived.

I left the next day, never to return, and never speaking to Sal again. I felt like I was running for my life, which meant leaving the past year, and everyone in it, behind me. Including the one real friend I had made in Fresno.

NEW BEGINNINGS

When I arrived in San Diego, I quickly found a place to crash with an old friend of mine who was living near a little beach town called Pacific Beach. It was close to the main office, which was great and just 2 days later, after settling in with the little I had brought with me, I started work in a new city.

Once again, Sal was right. The new office met me with open arms and immediately became my family. I felt safe and supported as they rallied around me. It was such a different place than Fresno. The people were friendlier, and everything was a bit more laid back.

In a short amount of time, I began making decent money selling insulation. I was able to get a small apartment, but I still didn't have quite enough to buy any furniture. I didn't care though. At least I wasn't sleeping on anyone's couch anymore. I had a place of my own with a roof over my head, and a job with people that encouraged and appreciated me.

I slept comfortably each night in my sleeping bag on the floor. Because I was on a tight budget, I ate a lot of cooked cabbage. No matter the circumstances, I felt a sense of deep gratitude that I was able to get away from the physical abuse when I did. Given everything that had happened, I often found myself looking over my shoulder, as trusting had become extremely difficult for me, and fear constantly consumed my thoughts. I had escaped madness and ended up in one of the most beautiful places on earth. I was surrounded by beautiful people, working a job that I was good at and liked enough to stay. It was a promising fresh start. Yet I could not seem to escape my mind and the thoughts that took up space, holding me back and keeping me small, afraid, and alone.

REFLECTION

What (or who) have you experienced in your life that has changed you? Was this change supportive? Do you need to revisit this part of your life, and possibly make some new, updated changes to support the YOU that is reading this now?

6

SEX, DRUGS AND MY LOST SOUL

Delirium's Hands

My eyes burn bright
At the promise of swift exodus
The steep dive through the shadows
To the cove and the sea

I'll slip from the binds
Of solitude and safety
I'd rather go mad
Than chatter and pretend

Dive and dive each night
Stagger through nothingness
Fall apart by noon
And swim away at dusk

I will live again
In delirium's hands
Uprooted from shame
From this pasture grey

- William Wright Jr.

From as far back as I can remember, I felt like an outsider, someone just looking through the picture window and watching other people live their lives. I wouldn't open the door to go in because I never felt like I fit in, and I couldn't take a chance of getting stuck there with people pointing and laughing at me. I felt as though I was walking around and seeing others, but I never felt like they really saw me. And when I did step out and try to connect, people didn't seem to understand me. It was like I was speaking a language that no one had ever heard of. I'd speak only to feel like my words were falling on deaf ears, or maybe it was that nobody cared what I had to say in the first place. Either way, I eventually found myself silently watching from the sidelines, my thoughts swirling in my mind, never being shared for fear of rejection or misunderstanding.

You might have felt this way at some point in your life, lost... alone... unseen. It's uncomfortable and often, confusing. And at times, it can seem impossible to change.

As a young adult, it became hard for me to connect deeply with people. The feeling of being so vulnerable felt scary as I was constantly afraid that if people saw my truth and my weaknesses, they'd judge me and eventually, push me aside. Like most people, I wanted to be liked! So instead of showing my full self and facing rejection, I continued to master an alter ego (my mask). This was the confident and strong side of myself that only showed the happy and positive Patricia, all the while masking my insecurities that had been embedded within since my youth.

Wearing a mask became normal for me, which helped me to only show the pieces of myself I wanted others to see while covering up the rest. These were the pieces that didn't feel as raw and real, which allowed me to keep myself safe (or so I thought). I hid my true emotions from the world, too afraid of my own truth which had become painful to admit. But buried below the surface was a young woman consumed by darkness and shame, and full of unbearable mental anguish that took over every fiber of my being.

Instead of letting others in to witness these parts of myself, I learned early on to shut these emotions off (long enough to seem normal, anyway) in order to make friends, all the while doing my best to deal with my inner turmoil on my own, in my own way. The truth was, I'd gotten so good at covering up my feelings that I began to see the world as a dark and scary place in which I needed to constantly protect myself from. All that did though was create more separation between the love I desired so deeply, and my reality. I had built walls instead of windows, keeping people close enough to seem like everything was fine, like I was fine... yet far enough away that I still felt like I was in control so nobody could hurt me.

I had mastered the art of earning people's trust and bullshitting my way into jobs, and even relationships, by using whatever means I knew to get me what I wanted. Putting on my daily mask became easier and easier. Each morning, as I would put on my makeup, I'd simply add "mask" to the list of products, and go about my day. I was in survival-mode, doing whatever I had to do to get through each day. On the inside though, I was always a flurry of emotions, which I allowed to surface behind closed doors where nobody could see. Whether it was by picking up a stray animal on the street to bring it to safety, or looking out for an elderly woman to make sure she got across the street okay, as long as those that "knew" me couldn't see the real me, I felt safe.

Here was the girl that wouldn't allow an animal, or elder to suffer, yet when confronted with everyday people, and/or relationships, I learned to show nothing but strength (and control). I didn't want to appear weak, or be seen as the vulnerable one, so I kept my mask on at all times in public as a way to prove that I was impenetrable. It was the only way I knew how to stay in control of my life. It became the only way I knew how to function and it would subsequently take a toll on me and all my relationships. Eventually, this warped way of thinking and showing up in the world left me completely alone and everytime I took off the mask in the privacy of my own home, the emptiness within would flood my body like an ocean storm swallowing a tiny ship at sea.

On the inside I wanted to have those beautiful relationships I saw others experiencing. I deeply desired to have deep conversations with people I cared about, and to fall in love just like I'd read about in all the romance novels. I wanted a love that never judged, complete with arms that would hold me through all my emotions, the ones I heard about as a kid in fairytales. And although I continued to seek that kind of love, and sometimes I would even get it for a period of time, the feelings were always fleeting. The moment I began to feel "too vulnerable" or exposed, I would run, too afraid to face the emotions that came with that kind of intimacy.

THE MASK OF (IM)PERFECTION

Imposter syndrome showed up in spades in my twenties. After I lost my job with the airlines, which I had turned into my identity, I felt like I'd lost everything and with that, I didn't think I had anything left to give.

Being fired hurt, and with that pain came a deep sense of lack and inadequacy. I had finally let my guard down and allowed myself to be vulnerable, and everything I had worked so hard for was taken from me. It wasn't just a job to me, it was an opportunity to dive into something bigger than myself - a purpose. It was also an opportunity to connect with people, and establish myself in a career that I was truly passionate about. Having it stripped away so quickly and unexpectedly left a void that I didn't know how to fill. Being a stewardess (or flight attendant, as they're called nowadays) allowed me to feel like part of a family for the first time, and I hated that it had been swept out from under me. That experience proved what I'd believed all along, I wasn't good enough - and maybe I never would be.

At the time, I hadn't realized the impact of it all. But looking back, losing that job sent me in such a downward spiral that I felt like I'd never be able to find my way out. It was like the earth had opened up to swallow me whole, and there I was with a shovel in hand, digging myself deeper and trying to escape the shame and embarrassment of how unlovable I was. I felt utterly worthless and this was proof that no matter how hard I tried, life was hard and I was destined to fail.

FAMILY SECRETS

After I escaped From Fresno to San Diego, I continued to work for the insulation company for about a year, until I finally lost interest and quit. I had taken up with the manager of the company who I liked a lot, and I felt it was exhilarating for a time to sneak around behind his fiancé's back, not thinking or caring about anyone else's feelings. He was nice to me and I enjoyed the lack of responsibility or commitment. I knew the rejection would eventually come, which meant I needed to leave before that happened, but I had to be the one in control, which meant leaving on my terms. This was how I approached just about everything. If things became uncomfortable, I would find a way to move on.

My life had been turned upside down and to add another layer to it all, I got some disturbing news while visiting my parents. I found my mom crying in her bedroom and when I asked her why she was crying, she hesitated. I could tell that whatever she was about to share was something she feared would upset me, but I needed to know. She indicated that my dad had been cheating on her for years, but that she had just let it go, and that she didn't want me to get involved. As appalled as I was, I wasn't shocked. It actually made a lot of things that I had questioned growing up make sense, Like when he would leave early from family vacations, or come home late after long hours at the office.

I took in what my mother told me, and for the first time, I began to understand her depression, and her drinking. I wanted to honor my mothers wishes and keep this secret between us, which I did. But I could never quite look at my father the same way again.

Finding out from my mom that the man I idolized, whose love I begged and pleaded for and was so proud of, had been screwing around on my mother (who was already a vulnerable woman) was devastating. The man whose words I believed. The man I respected, who portrayed the very attributes of the kind of person I thought I wanted to be was a total asshole! And apparently I was just like him. Turns out, the apple didn't fall far from the tree. For years I wanted to be just like him, and so with practice, and a lot of fake smiles, I became him. And now all I wanted to do was wash everything about myself that was like him away.

There was so much anger within me, which I tried to mute through drinking, drugs and men, especially at night when I was alone and feeling sorry for myself. I used whatever I could to mask the pain, and pretend it didn't exist, if only temporarily. I thought that if I didn't get involved with anyone too deeply, I wouldn't feel any emotions, and if I didn't show or feel emotions, I couldn't get hurt. I saw my friends go through break-ups and be hurt and vulnerable, and that was surely not what I wanted. I was great at listening and consoling them, I just didn't want to feel any of that myself.

I believed from a young age that I was unlovable, and so to prove my biases, I would set myself up to be rejected before I had a chance to be accepted. I would find ways to stop communicating with a new boyfriend, or even friends because I knew if I stayed too long, then one would surely find my faults, see that I was a fake, and leave me. I had to be in control, which meant controlling my own outcomes no matter how detrimental doing so might be to my life.

Over the next several years, I lived in a world of short-lived relationships, never giving people the time to get to know the real me. I would reject before I was rejected, which only got worse after the rapes.

Contrary to how I may have come across, I didn't have a cold heart. In fact, it was quite the opposite. I felt emotions hard, I just wouldn't allow them to show on the outside. I believed that being strong meant keeping it all together and neglecting to openly share my true feelings with the world around me. It was the only way I could manage to protect myself from being hurt ever again, no matter what.

MUSIC TO MY GUARDED HEART

I had been in San Diego for some time when my friend, Jennifer, a beautiful Armenian musician and singer in a local band, asked me if I wanted to go to a club with her one night.

I hadn't been out for a while and music had always been an outlet to fill the void in my wandering, lost soul. Music made it easier to escape and tune out the world that I found so painful. I also had a bit of extra money and thought it would be fun to dress up and get out of the house for once (I'd remained pretty reclusive up to this point).

We scheduled a time to meet at the entrance of Crystal T's, a well-known disco club, for dancing. I was excited as I began to get ready, pulling out my blue wrap skirt that easily slid around my slim body, along with a form fitting black leotard top that followed my curves. My sun-drenched blonde hair, highlighted naturally from being at the beach regularly, hung sensually just below my shoulders.

I looked at myself in the mirror as I stepped into my colorful platform shoes, which made me inches taller than I actually was, twisting my torso back and forth, feeling happy with what I saw. I then took the time to carefully separate my long lashes with midnight blue mascara that made my steel blue eyes stand out before outlining my lips with my favorite bright red lipstick so they would appear flawless. I had become almost masterful at accentuating my best features, thanks to my modeling stint when I was in my teens. I felt sexy, and ready for a fun night out on the town.

I saw Jennifer standing at the door waiting for me, tall and lean with legs that went on forever. She looked stunning with her dark skin, and long black hair that seemed to glow as the sun began to set. We were quite opposite in looks, but both stood out in our own way when we were together. She must have arrived early, as I was never late, a trait my father had instilled in me. I hurried over to her, waving my hand as she smiled with acknowledgment. As soon as I reached her, we both headed through the tall crystal doors together, giggling with great anticipation of what the night might bring.

The club did not disappoint, it was swarming with beautiful men and women, with their gold chains, and sexy outfits. The lights were low and the music was loud. I will never forget the song, "I feel good" by James Brown playing as I dragged Jennifer out onto the dance floor. Everyone was dancing with everyone, and the energy in the room was electrifying. I felt my body swaying, the music permeating my ears, as the lights flickered like small crystals. It was an immediate escape from the hardships and darkness of the day. Or more accurately, the darkness of my life.

We finished dancing after several songs, and walked up to the long low-lit bar where there were two empty stools positioned together at the end. We ordered margaritas with salt, while tapping our toes to the beat of the music. I danced to every song with a different guy that night, while Jennifer sat cozied up in a booth with a man she'd met earlier in the evening. I was happy sitting on a bar stool, sipping drinks, and dancing the night away. The music always made me feel good, and was a welcomed release from my overthinking mind. That night I wasn't looking for anyone, just an escape into another land, which I found.

Christal T's became my favorite club at least four nights a week. And Jacob, the bartender, always saved the exact same stool for me. Him and I would chat when it was slow, and I would sip on whatever new cocktail he would create for me to test, while dancing between sips. It was one of my favorite hangouts, a place I could go on my own, and feel comfortable and safe.

Eventually I would meet guys, sometimes just dancing, other times, through long, slow kisses. And there were also the times where dancing led to me going home with a man I felt a physical chemistry with. It was never something that needed to be discussed for in these instances, it was just assumed there would be a hookup. One-night stands didn't phase me, as I'd gotten so good at numbing myself and viewing sex or any kind of physical intimacy as nothing more than a pleasurable pasttime.

Men found me sexy, and I liked that they would hover and were attentive for a night of dancing, and surface level conversation. On these nights, I felt like I mattered and that's all I wanted. They never asked for a phone number after a night of unbridled, and uninhibited sex. And there were no expectations on either side. It was just a silent understanding of sexual freedom that I invited in with open arms, and a closed heart.

There were times where guys would offer me cocaine, which I would often accept. I would get high in the bathroom, or we'd slip out a side door and take a few lines together along with some kissing or more illicit sexual favors. I even had what they called a "pinky image," which was a solid gold fake nail that was attached to my pinky finger which was used to snort coke.

I was reckless, and it felt freeing.

I changed jobs and moved several times, mostly by the beach because the beach was a place I always felt at peace. Listening to the rolling waves soothed my soul and became a temporary escape before heading to one of the many jobs I bounced around to and from throughout that period of my life.

I worked as a sales associate in a store by the beach selling bathing suits for a few years and as a food delivery girl driving a food truck to nearby construction sites to feed the workers, and to keep the tip jar overflowing. I would wear my shortest hot pants which brought in good tips, and allowed me to continue spending my days hanging out at the beach to get a tan before heading out once again for a night of clubbing, drugs and meaningless sex.

If I did date, it would only be for a month or so, in which case I would buy the guy things, and literally put myself into debt trying to please whoever it was that week, thinking that by showering him with gifts, it would make him like me more. When that didn't work, or I felt too vulnerable, I would dump him, or the man-of-the-hour would just quit calling. I told myself that *love was for someone else, not for me*. But all of these behaviors left me feeling empty, worthless and more ashamed.

This pattern continued for several years. Different clubs with different guys, on and off. I would take speed to feel productive, enjoying the revved up feeling it gave me. It was the same feeling that coke provided, which I loved, only less expensive.

I spent years being sexually promiscuous, doing drugs and being soulless. I chose shitty partners and refused to connect with anyone because what was the point? I had learned to only trust myself, and even that was shaky at times. I played the victim, and I played it very well. But in doing so, I had lost the essence of who I was deep within. My soul had become a sea of chaos and darkness, and I had no desire to get out for that meant feeling the pain I'd worked so hard to stuff inside and that was not an option.

At this point, I wasn't really speaking to my parents much, unless I really needed something. I would turn on the charm and my dad would always come through. I knew how to play him for money, and I even got him to give me my moms car after mine had been repossessed.

I had gone so far down the rabbit (shit) hole that it was hard to dig myself out. However, I still considered myself lucky in so many ways. The Universe must have been looking out for me as somehow I was able to manage my job, and my life, without becoming a complete drug addict, after so many years of over-abuse. I apparently was blessed with what some professionals might call, "a non-addictive personality." Although that didn't make my behavior "healthy" or right by any means.

I was always surprised at the control I had. I found that when I truly rooted myself and made a decision, my willpower could be relentless. When I wanted something, or I really wanted to learn something new, nothing could stop me. This gave me a feeling of power, and although that feeling only lasted momentarily, I loved being in control of my life.

MASKING PAIN WITH BEAUTY

Over the next few months, I made the decision to stop hitting the clubs every night and instead, only went with friends on the weekends. I would still meet guys and do coke, but it became less and less important to me, as I wanted to get back into fashion, something that had always interested me. I loved clothes and cosmetics, and I enjoyed looking good.

I decided to interview for a cosmetic position at Robinsons in the Fashion Valley Mall and true to form, I was hired instantly to be the Elizabeth Arden Representative in Cosmetics. This made me happy, and gave my confidence a little boost. I was excited to try something new that I enjoyed again. I was helping women feel better about themselves, which I guess was my way of using my pain for good. I had an eye for designing makeup on a myriad of faces and it felt great to see women walking out of the department store with the kind of confidence I wished I had. While I was helping to make others feel more beautiful, I was stuck with my own inner turmoil. I could feel the ugliness of the lies and self-sabotage I was still holding onto suffocating me.

It didn't take long before I fell in love with my work. In fact, I loved it so much that I talked my parents into giving me enough money to go to cosmetology school to become a professional makeup artist and licensed California esthetician. When I enjoyed something and applied myself, I excelled. It was easy for me to be at the top of the class and pass tests with flying colors, which made me feel unstoppable.

I began to realize that I had more control over my life than I thought. Which meant that somehow, maybe I could actually change the trajectory of where I was headed after all.

REFLECTION

Do you feel like you are wearing a mask at times, and pretending to be someone you're not? What would it feel like to be free of the mask, and courageously express yourself to the world? What's stopping you?

7

BETRAYAL, MANIPULATION, AND CONTROL

Love is patient,
Love is kind.
It does not envy,
It does not boast,
It is not proud.
It does not dishonor others,
It is not self-seeking,
It is not easily angered,
It keeps no record of wrongs.
Love does not delight in evil,
But rejoices with the truth.
It always protects,
Always trusts,
Always hopes
Always perseveres.
Love never fails.

1 Corinthians 13:4-8

I turned and stopped in my tracks as my palms began to sweat, and my heart began to pound. There he stood, on the other side of Chrystal T's dance floor, standing and talking with some other guys who appeared to be friends of his. As he spoke, his smiling eyes captivated me, and I couldn't look away. I watched him as he turned towards me slightly, obviously feeling my stare penetrating him and even still, I could not stop gawking. There was a magnetic energy about him that drew me in from across the room. He was of average height with dark, wavy hair, which fell easily around the back of his neck. His clothes were trendy and he appeared to have a European flair about him. I knew in an instant that he would be someone special in my life.

As I continued to stare, his eyes met mine, and I could feel everything within me melt. Part of me wanted to become invisible, but I also knew I had to meet him. I couldn't dismiss this intuitive feeling for my inner knowing was strong and I had learned to trust my gut without needing a proper explanation. So I took a deep breath and mustered the courage necessary before walking towards him. I noticed that he had leaned in to say something to his friends before he turned to walk in my direction. My body was pulsating, and I swore he could see my hands shaking from the nerves. His eyes were so kind, and his smile was warm. Everything about him put me at ease in an instant. It was as if I was home, without ever speaking a word to him. The knowing was fierce, as was my attraction and desire to connect. As he moved closer, he reached out his hand and without hesitation, I put mine in his as he gently pulled me onto the dance floor. It felt easy, and somehow, familiar.

When the song finished, another song began, this time slow. He pulled me closer to him as we began to sway, which made me feel both weak and safe all at the same time. As he placed his head closer to mine I could feel his warm breath as he whispered into my ear with an accent that I couldn't quite identify, "What's your name?" I could barely get my words out. "Patricia," I said. "That's a beautiful name. It's nice to meet you, Patricia. My name is Jared." In that moment, everything in my body dissolved, and I felt my heart opening as our body's moved in sync under the dim club lights.

Jared and I danced together for the rest of the night. The conversation flowed easily, and by last call, instead of assuming we would go home together, he walked me to my car like a gentleman. Before closing the door, he asked me for my phone number and let me know that he'd like to take me to brunch on Sunday. This was new for me, unknown territory, and I felt like a young blushing school girl standing in front of her first crush. Yet everything seemed so right. After giving him my number and agreeing to go out with him, I drove away dreaming of the next time I'd see this man who'd swept me off my feet.

Old Patterns Die Hard

Just as he'd promised, Jared picked me up promptly on Sunday morning and took me to a beautiful restaurant that overlooked the water. We talked and drank mimosa's for several hours. Time flew by that day and although we'd only just met, I knew he was different. And I was right, because as it turns out, that chance meeting was the beginning of what would become one of my greatest love stories.

After that perfect first date, we spent almost every day and night together for months, until eventually, we moved in together.

I believe Jared saved my life. He was different from the other guys I'd dated, which I didn't realize I'd needed. He drank socially, and only smoked occasionally - and he didn't do drugs. He was a Civil Engineer of Lebanese descent and spoke several languages and at the time, he was studying for his master's degree.

He was smart, kind, sexy and he definitely kept my attention. His family was Muslim, and very forward thinking, which I appreciated. And although I knew from the moment I saw him across the dance floor that he would be a special person in my life, I also knew somewhere inside that he would not be my *forever person*. Marriage was never something we talked about, but I think that was because we both knew the truth. Although we loved each other, it would not be enough to keep us together given our extremely different cultural backgrounds. Instead of discussing our future, we remained focused on the time we had together, which more often than not, was incredibly fulfilling. I believed then (as I do now) that our paths crossed for a reason, one of which was his positive influence on my party girl lifestyle. I believe that had I continued down the path I was on before meeting him, it would've killed me. Jared saved me from that demise. In return, I was able to provide a real sense of our American culture, something he yearned to better understand and experience.

There was no judgement with Jared, and I loved that I could always be myself. But there was a subtle feeling of control that I felt from him on occasion, which left me wary at times. Understandably, because of my past relationships with men, I was a bit more sensitive to this. Plus, growing up with a controlling father I knew all too well what this kind of behavior could turn into. I was also very aware of my tendency to easily overreact at times, often rebelling and putting up walls when I felt or thought someone was trying to steal my freedom and from time to time, this pattern showed up between us.

To put this in context, when I found out that my sister was dying from cancer, I wanted and needed to go home to see her. Despite this being something very important to me, I felt pressure from Jared to stay home with him instead of being there with the most important person in my life while she lay in pain. He didn't want me to leave him so I convinced myself that he wanted me to choose between him and my sister (although he never used those words), which angered me. And honestly, that was not even an option because my sister would always be my first choice, no matter what.

I was extremely upset with him, and realized later that he hadn't quite understood the extent of her sickness, nor the fact that she was dying. But my ego was reacting as it typically did when I felt like someone was trying to control me. When this happened, I would flip the script and try to control the situation instead to protect myself and stay in the driver's seat. I could be very stubborn, and found it really hard to listen when I felt this way. The moment that I felt that anyone was trying to silence me, or control my path, I would begin to pull back. It was a continuous pattern in my life, one in which I chose not to see (or admit) for a long time.

GOODBYE, SWEET GINGER

My sister's death was rather sudden, as she hid her symptoms from the family until it was no longer possible for her to hide them any longer. Once the cancer had taken over, the prognosis was bleak. My mother took her to chemo every day for a few months. Meanwhile, we remained hopeful and optimistic as there were good days thrown in with the bad, too. My sister had sent me a beautifully handwritten note dated June 13th, which said she was getting better, and that her "white cells were winning" and she felt she would beat the infection. But not long after, on July 11th, she passed away. My whole world was turned upside down. The thread to my family was already thin, and now it was quickly unravelling. I had no idea how to go on without her for she was my lifeline, and my voice when I felt I had none. She nurtured me when my soul was hurting, and she always knew what to say and do to put me at ease. I was alone, and nothing would ever be the same again without my sweet sister, Ginger by my side to confide in.

Healing took time but eventually, I accepted that she'd want me to move on and enjoy my life. I could hear her telling me, "You must go on Pod, I am counting on you. I love you and will always be with you." And she is, every single day. I feel her presence as if she's right next to me, like my very own angel attached to my side. This gives me a sense of peace and I am often overcome by gratitude at the thought of the bond we shared. Not everyone gets that, and I know I was lucky to have her here while I did.

I needed to be better for her. She had kept me hopeful and strong for so many years, it was time I learned to do this on my own for myself, and for her. We had such a special connection in life and even in death, it remains strong. Her soul lives on within me, and always will. I knew the day would come when I could honestly say, "Look, Ginger, I did it!" It didn't happen overnight by any means, but I was committed to making her proud while I was alive, even though physically, she was gone.

I know that Jared never meant to hold me back from my sister, but I refused to let it go. That one negative experience prevented me from moving closer to him. Instead, it caused me to retreat inward, and a distance was created between us. Something that would fester for many years after.

New Beginnings

The relationship we had, while flawed (as relationships tend to be), was a good one. For many years, he was kind and supportive, and we loved one another deeply. The reality was, however, that we both knew that our cultures were too far apart and it was inevitable that our values would collide down the road. And 7 year later, they did.

Up to that point, we respected and admired each other. I can honestly say that he was the first man that really cared for me, and I felt it. But like so many things in life, it was not meant to last. I will always be grateful for his love, and the fact that he saved me from myself. Besides our differences, and the knowing within that our love was not meant to be the kind that spanned decades, Jared could not have been my forever love, anyway. Because somewhere inside, I always knew that my heart belonged to someone else, my first love, whom I had met at the impressionable age of 16 years old.

His name was Peter. He was an older boy that lived in my neighborhood growing up, who I finally got to notice me one summer before he headed off to college. Even though he ended up leaving me only to become engaged and later married to someone else, I continued to love him, and I believed with all of my heart and soul that I would marry him some day. When people would ask me, "Why don't you marry Jared?" I would say, "Because I am going to marry Peter!" It seemed silly, I knew this. But as I said, my gut instinct was strong and as proof, 22 years later, Peter and I rekindled our relationship - and we got married! Something I truly thought I'd always wanted.

A word to the wise: Be careful what you wish for (and what you choose to manifest). Because like me, you just might get it.

Young Lust: A Recipe For Disaster

I was 16, naïve, and had fallen in puppy love with Peter, the neighborhood boy who would drive to his best friend's house almost daily, which happened to be directly across the street from my house. I saw him in his white car, blonde, and tan with a smile that lit up my heart. I fell in love almost instantly and at 16, I tried everything to get him to notice me, doing cartwheels in my yard when he drove by, or walking past his friend's house when I knew he was there playing basketball. I was just a young girl longing to love and be loved. And finally, it worked!

It was the summer before he left for college, and I was about to enter my junior year of highschool. I was a scrawny girl that had finally grown into her body and Peter, who was 3 years older than me, finally took notice. Ours was a beautiful summer of sweet kisses, beach outings, and hand holding. He found me funny and energetic, and that was enough for me to fall madly in love. He could do no wrong in my eyes. He was respectful, cute, and he wrote me love letters. I just knew he would be the man I would someday marry.

Peter left to go to college that Fall, and everything was wonderful... until the letters began to lessen, and the phone calls subsided. And then at Christmas, when people had come home for the holidays, I heard he was engaged to someone he had met at college. I was heartbroken! Yet something inside me said, *it's not your time, just be patient... you will marry him someday, Patricia.* For whatever reason, I really believed this, too.

We were polar opposites in many ways, but don't opposites attract? That's what I told myself. It never even occurred to me that we might not be compatible, and the thought certainly didn't cross my mind to question whether we should even get married in the first place. I just knew it's what I wanted (at 16!), and so it would be.

It may have taken 22 years, but the Universe must have heard my pleas loud and clear because when Peter and I reconnected all those years later, there was no question in my mind that this was it. The problem was, my patterns hadn't changed much. Not in the way I needed them to in order to spot the red flags and know when to walk away.

Looking back, those red flags were as obvious as the nose on my face, but I refused to see them. He was my Peter, my fantasy, my first love. He was perfect in my eyes, and to me, he could do no wrong.

The wedding was everything I'd ever dreamed it would be! All of our friends were there from 20 years prior, and they couldn't believe their eyes either. It was a fairytale story coming true and I was the princess of the ball.

Unfortunately, our fairytale was short-lived and just 3 years into the marriage, I knew I had made a terrible mistake. He was not the baby-faced "perfect" man I remembered at all. He had gone to a very upscale school, whereas I hadn't finished college, and he would use his intellect to put me down, and make me feel worthless. He loved my energy, and I allowed him to drain it from me every chance he got. His mood swings were erratic and unpredictable and he could go days, even weeks without speaking to me. He was never physically abusive, but the mental abuse and his controlling side almost felt worse. Bones heal, but words kill your inner worth, and just like that, I was back to not feeling good enough all over again. I spent so many years teetering along a delicate balance of feeling good and then allowing people to bring me down. It was a constant roller coaster that I couldn't seem to escape from and the only thing I knew to do was to hide, and try to figure things out on my own.

This marriage was hell and it was obvious that I'd made a massive mistake walking back into our puppy love relationship from so many years earlier. I was ashamed. How could I tell anyone that the love of my life, of over 20 years, was not the man I thought he was? My fantasy had burst and I felt humiliated. The problem for me was that now my sister was gone, which meant that I didn't have anyone I could talk to.

I found myself spiraling down the path of old negative behaviors. I was embarrassed, and I felt so stupid! Why couldn't I get it right? My inner dialogue was mean, and terribly judgemental. I wanted to be somewhere else - anywhere else but here.

I began to drink again, spending money that I knew I didn't have and about 7 years into the marriage, I started having affairs to escape and kill the pain. My default had always been to run whether to someone or something else as my way of hiding and masking reality. Right or wrong, this pattern made me feel a surge of empowerment and although it only lasted briefly each time, I kept telling myself that this time would be different... this time, things would actually change (even if I had not).

When it came to the affairs, I never understood or cared about the heartbreak that I was leaving in my wake. This was my shadow side coming out, and I did what I wanted, while also ensuring to cover up the mess. I couldn't take the chance of being caught. I had become what I hated - a heartless philanderer on the outside while on the inside, the shame, fear and guilt were killing me slowly every day. I hated myself, but I didn't know how to stop.

ONTO THE NEXT

Eventually, one of my affairs turned into my second marriage. Bill was funny, smart and he made me laugh. I mean, roll on the floor laugh until my sides hurt. That is what drew me to him in the first place, and I loved that about him. We had some very good years together, but he had a very big ego and in my typical fashion, I became less available (mentally) and he needed a lot of attention. I was consumed with work, making a lot of money (and spending a lot more), thinking that giving him material things would buy me love. But I didn't appreciate him, and of course, looking back he had his own past that he'd brought with him, which I should've seen coming. I seemed to be blinded by my incessant need for immediate satisfaction, never looking beyond the present moment to acknowledge the truth of the matter in front of me.

He had left his wife for me, and I had left "the love of my life" for him. And because I didn't know how to fix things, anytime anything went wrong, I would run. I was right on track with my patterns and like clock-work, it would eventually bite me in the ass.

Looking back, the fact that I never saw conflict in my own family growing up (it was always hidden from us) wasn't healthy. In fact, it caused me to believe that if something wasn't working, then the best thing for me to do was just remove myself from the situation instead of working together to resolve it.

Conflict was upsetting to me, and the thought of working through conflict with others was not a concept I understood. I not only hated conflict, but I hated confrontation even more. It never occurred to me that you needed to work on things in relationships to maintain them. But confrontation and conflict equaled pain in my eyes and the idea that you could have healthy conflict and confrontation made no sense to me at the time. The only thing I understood was that if it felt hard, I didn't like it, and I didn't want to be part of it.

There were so many mixed messages growing up that the thought of living life the way others did was confusing to me, so I just did what I knew instead. Hide and run became my motto, and it's how I operated in every aspect of my life for decades.

Each time I ran and started a new life, everything would be fine for a period of time. Many people call it the 'honeymoon period,' and I liked it there! (I think we all do, though.) As soon as there were any signs of things going south, I would get scared and want to run. I had no idea how to fix the real problems at hand and so my unhealthy behaviors would rear their sneaky little heads, which meant my results repeated themselves over and over again as well.

The only difference with Bill was that he was the one who ran and strayed first. I knew in my gut he was seeing someone, but I refused to believe it, so I covered it up. I would make up excuses for him to my friends about why he wasn't around because I didn't want to face the obvious and what I knew deep within to be true.

This went on for about a year and half until his "girlfriend" (whom he'd been seeing on the side) started taunting me with weird phone calls and emails, which I tried to ignore. But there was one particular email I couldn't let go. She sent me pictures of them together and I lost it! Sometimes, when things are out of sight, they're also out of mind. But when it's thrown in your face, there's nowhere to hide and you can't ignore it. I had no choice but to admit what was happening, and give up all the excuses I'd made. This was it, my last straw. And not only was my marriage over (again), but I was left to pick up the pieces of my past and make a decision as to how I would proceed and change the trajectory I was on from toxic to something that felt good.

REFLECTION

Do you feel stuck, often finding it hard to accept (receive) love? What would it feel like to allow yourself to receive such a gift? What's stopping you?

8

LOSING IT ALL TO FIND MYSELF

Love After Love

The time will come, when with elation,
you will greet yourself arriving
at your own door, in your own mirror,
and each will smile at the other's welcome
and say, sit here. Eat.
You will love again the stranger who was yourself.
Give wine. Give bread. Give back your heart
to itself, to the stranger who has loved you.
all your life, whom you have ignored for another, who knows you by heart.
Take down the love letters from the bookshelf,
the photographs, the desperate notes,
peel your own image from the mirror.
Sit. Feast on your life.

- Derek Walcott

Where was all this wisdom I am supposed to gain with age? I couldn't seem to get off the merry-go-round. Instead, I kept going up and down and round and round, repeating the same mistakes over and over again. I continued to wake up and put on my lipstick as I stuffed each problem, trauma and mistake into that

74

proverbial suitcase I'd been carrying around, which kept expanding and getting heavier as time went on. For some reason, I just couldn't put that ripped and ratty old baggage down! Maybe it was comfort. Maybe it was fear. Maybe it was both. All I knew was that it was heavy, and it was weighing me down.

By this point not only had my sister died, but my mother had as well. All of that loss along with the demise of my second marriage. And just when I thought I might be able to heal my past once and for all, the world slapped me in the face again.

The recession had hit hard in the Real Estate industry, and at that particular time, I had already been on a downward trend when it came to making money. By this time, my successful real estate career was on a slippery slope towards nonexistence, and I had gotten myself into deep debt. It began to look like there may be no way out this time.

The rabbit hole of destructive behavior was taunting me to go for another ride and go back to my days of alcohol and cocaine use. And because I was weak (and more than that, deathly afraid), I began to let my old shitty habits lead the way. My imbalanced self-worth was back on the floor and I was headed toward rock bottom. I just didn't know how to catch myself this time as it felt like there were no handles to grab onto. In a way, it was almost comforting, wallowing in my sorrow, feeling like a victim, playing the old record that asked, *why does this always happen to me?*

It all seemed to happen so quickly. This particular downward spiral started pretty quickly after my mom's death. I felt like a complete orphan, not only mentally alone, but physically alone too. By a wild stretch of the imagination, I thought my husband would be there for me during my mom's passing but that was not the case. I held onto that hope for about a week, but he couldn't support me. The truth was, I was in a loveless marriage, without any money coming in and I was on the verge of losing everything (mentally and materialistically). Not to mention being 40 pounds overweight.

As my marriage disintegrated before my eyes, I continued lying to myself and others for months about my husband's whereabouts. And to mask my own pain and feelings of unworthiness, I began dangerously hooking up with men online, thinking it would help validate me in one way or another. But it only made me feel worse. To complicate things further, I began drowning my sorrows at night in a sea of martini's, wine, and occasionally, a bump or two of cocaine to numb myself from everything and everyone around me.

Everything I knew to be true in my life was crashing down around me. I told myself that no one loved me, and convinced myself that I simply didn't matter. On the outside, I was doing what I'd learned to do which was to hold things together, at least enough to give people the impression that everything was fine. But it was all a bunch of fucking bullshit and deep down, I knew better.

I felt empty inside. I had lost it all - my money, my husband, myself - and for what? What was the point of even going on if I had nothing to show for any of it? I told myself that life was not on my side, and for whatever reason, I couldn't seem to get the toxic behavior under control to change things. Even the simplest of things felt heavy and I wanted to quit. One minute I'd be laughing, smiling, feeling good, and seemingly on top of the world... and the next, I was drunk and ugly crying with mascara running down my cheeks, red lipstick smeared all over my face, while curled up on my expensive penthouse floor.

I was a complete mess.

BRILLIANCE IN THE MIDST OF BELLIGERENCE

It was a cool September night, which had started off like most other nights. I was sitting on my couch, feeling sorry for myself with my 2 cats snuggled up against me, watching mindless TV with a fresh martini in hand. But on this particular night, I'd had an extra martini, the one that when I did overindulge on occasion, would put me over the edge, and I started to sob. I felt so alone, so worthless, so lost, with no visible hope in sight. I didn't feel like I had the energy to see another day and it was clear that things could not get any worse.

I laid there alone, crying on the floor for what seemed like hours. My body hurt, and the floor was wet from my endless tears, when suddenly I felt something touch me softly on the back of my hand. As I turned my head slightly to see what it was, I saw my cat, Hula (my 11 year old tabby with the largest green eyes I'd ever seen) staring at me. My lashes were soaking wet, and my vision was blurred from hours of sobbing (and possibly the martini's). As I stared back at her, I could feel her looking into my soul. As she placed her paw on my hand, I felt an energy pulsing through my body, and I could've sworn she was speaking to me through her eyes.

Yes, I'd been drinking. But I had a deep knowing inside that Hula was trying to tell me something important. It was an energy that I'd never felt before followed by the unspoken, yet deeply felt words, "Don't give up... you are needed! It's time to take your power back... I love you."

These words consumed my entire being like an echo chamber.

The surge of energy was warm and began to move from my hand, slowly penetrating every cell in my body. And as I sat with the sensations, five words came to my mind. I didn't understand why at the time, but I had the urge to grab a piece of paper and write them down.

Acknowledgement.
Forgiveness.
Mindset.
Accountability.
Perseverance.

As I lifted the pen from the paper and stared at the words, they made no sense to me. Yet I somehow knew that these five words were going to change (and possibly, save) my life.

CHOOSING TO LIVE

Right then and there, I realized I had a choice, and that was to get off the floor and get to work. It was time to change my life, and do whatever it took to stop playing the victim. No more excuses! This was my opportunity to take my power back, and choose myself, like *really* choose myself, for once. I had reached rock bottom and as hard as it was for me to admit, I was fucked up. I couldn't continue down this path any longer. It was killing me and one thing had become blatantly clear: if I didn't change my life right now, I wouldn't be here much longer.

That energy renewed me. I felt a new optimism about my life, and the world around me, believing in the endless possibilities available that I had closed my eyes to for so long. I was stronger than I had been giving myself credit for, and for far too long, I'd been making excuses for all the bullshit I was allowing in my life, including my poor decisions that led to a mediocre existence.

As I looked over and kissed Hula, I felt my sister's presence, as we both loved cats. And I knew that in her own jokester way, she was showing up in Hula as a way to get my attention. She was telling me that she loved me and that I had always made her proud, but enough was enough. It was time to get off the floor, and stop feeling sorry for myself. It was time for me to show myself and the world that I was a gift, and worthy of love and belonging because I was alive, nothing more or less.

It was such a powerful moment for me, and although I was full of booze and blow, barely coherent, my sister's presence was undeniable. Our connection had always been so strong, and somehow when it came to my sister, I could sense her in these moments, which I always trusted. The last time I could recall feeling my sister this strongly was when I flew home to see her prior to her death.

SEEING THE SIGNS

My mother had called to tell me that my sister had taken a turn for the worse, and even with all the chemo, they didn't think she was going to make it. I booked my ticket immediately after getting off the phone, and made it to Seattle just one day before she passed away. Whether conscious or not, it was a feeling and I followed it, and I'll forever be grateful I did.

On that trip home, my first leg to Seattle had a stop in Portland, Oregon, and I was feeling very anxious about seeing my sister. I was sitting in the middle of the plane when a priest got on in full robe and passed me with a smile. A feeling of relaxation came over me, and I just knew my sister would be okay until I got there.

When we landed in Portland a few hours later, the priest got off, and my heart sank. I knew something was wrong, and all I could think was that my beloved sister must be dying. It felt like the longest layover ever and I prayed in silence as I waited for the second leg of my journey to Seattle. As the Portland passengers started to board, I was feeling depressed and scared. But as I looked up, a sister in full habit walked down the aisle. As she passed me, she smiled and said hello, sitting down in the seat directly behind me. I felt a sense of peace wash over me, and I knew that Ginger would make it, at least until I got there to say goodbye.

Just like my experience with Hula in my drunken stupor, I knew that none of this was a coincidence. These religious figures were there to give me a sign, as you don't normally see religious persons traveling in their full formal wear. Someone wanted me to notice, and I did.

When the plane arrived in Seattle, a friend of my sisters picked me at the airport and took me directly to the hospital. As she was driving she let me know that about an hour before I landed, Ginger almost died. She had been struggling with her breathing for about 20 minutes, but she miraculously seemed to relax and stabilize, which also happened to be the very moment in Portland when the priest got off the plane, and the sister in full habit got on.

I made it to my sister's side that day, knowing that she had waited for me to get there. After several hours of being by her side, friends and family told me I should go home and get some sleep, and to come back in the morning. But I couldn't leave. I had traveled to be with her, and there was no way I was leaving her side, or the hospital for that matter. And then it happened. At two o'clock on the morning of July 11, 1982, Ginger passed away in my arms.

I am confident that my sister came to me through Hula on that drunken night for a reason, just as she had years prior when I was guided home to Seattle just in time to be with her as she took her last breath. The difference was that this time, I was being guided home to myself. And I was being told to get my shit together because my time was not up... I still had so many things left to do.

Signs are everywhere (apparently even in our pets!). It's not whether or not they exist, but whether or not we're willing to listen and honor them that makes all the difference.

WORDS MATTER

I studied the words I had written down in my drunken state and allowed myself to really feel them. I had stuffed so much baggage deep inside myself for so many years that they had exploded into all different parts of my daily life. I was $140,000 in debt, and I wasn't opening bills, or taking care of my responsibilities. I had been reckless and complacent for too long in my relationships, and had put my health on the back-burner. I had allowed people to take my power from me, giving all that I had, never taking the time to refill my own bucket. I was literally pouring whatever I had left into others as a way to seek validation and approval from the outside world. What I needed, however, was to give all of that love to myself and learn to love and accept myself without the opinions of others.

The day that Hula spoke to me was the very day that everything changed. I was no longer willing to live the way I had been for decades. Instead, I decided that I was ready to finally reclaim my power and remember who I was, and why I was here in the first place.

I took those five words to heart. I began acknowledging my darkness (my shadow self) and choosing acceptance and gratitude over judgement and shame. I began to acknowledge my faults and flaws, which was not easy to do. I chose to be brave with my story and figure out how to use it to fuel me forward in a healthy way. This time would be different because I refused to stay where I was any longer. And while it was hard and uncomfortable, I knew it was necessary if I wanted to make the changes necessary to live the life I knew was possible. I knew I had to feel the hurt in order to heal, and get really honest about everything I'd been pushing down inside.

Below is just a snippet of the process I went through as I chose better - and chose myself. I'm sharing this in hopes that it will support your journey home to yourself as well.

5 LITTLE (LIFE-CHANGING) WORDS

#1 - ACKNOWLEDGEMENT

By acknowledging my flaws and being completely honest with myself, I was able to:

1. Pay off the $140,000 debt I had accumulated.
2. Lose 40 pounds.
3. Change my negative behaviors that were sabotaging my life.
4. Build confidence.
5. Look myself in the mirror and be proud of what I saw.

#2 - FORGIVENESS

This word was hard, but it was necessary. Know that if this is something for you to work on as well, it might take some time, and that's okay. I understood that in order to live in the present moment and also honor my future, I needed to take the energy that I was giving to being angry at others back. I needed to choose more empowering emotions and thoughts, which also meant forgiving myself in the process. I did this by writing down the names and situations that I was holding onto and forgiving each one by saying, " I forgive you for, you know not what you do. You have your own story, and I wish you strength that you can forgive yourself just as I forgive you." I even added my own name to that list.

#3 - MINDSET

Once I acknowledged my faults, and really forgave the people I felt had hurt me, the negative energy released and my mindset began to shift. I started seeing my life from a different perspective, and cultivated a mindset with no limits - a mindset of growth. I continued this practice daily, using affirmations and celebrating my successes, big and small. I still do this to this day.

#4 - ACCOUNTABILITY

I learned that I needed to be accountable to myself. The more I held myself accountable, the more micro-goals I wrote down and was able to check off. And with that, the more my confidence grew and the future began looking brighter and brighter every day.

#5 - PERSEVERANCE

When I trusted the process and allowed it to work in my favor, I felt such relief. It became freeing, and it felt good. I also reminded myself to take one day at a time, and kept coming back to the truth that I had choices and I was in charge of the direction I was choosing. I *chose* not to give up and over time, it became easier and easier to persevere, even in the tough moments.

These 5 words changed me. And they opened me up in ways I'd only ever dreamed of. I ended up adding in my own 6th word (which I would encourage you to adopt as well) and that was: **Gratitude**. I learned that being grateful is not just a statement, but it is a word with deep meaning. For me it meant not simply being grateful for the car, the money, or the next thing I could buy. But being grateful for the world around me including the roof over my head, the food on my plate, the birds chirping, and my cat who makes me smile. Anything else is just a bonus.

While the healing process was dreadfully confronting and uncomfortable, choosing to embrace it and step into it fully saved me. I faced my fears head on, and continued choosing myself at every turn. It was not easy. It was not a quick process. And it was not exactly "fun." But now looking back from the other side of it all, I can say with certainty that it was absolutely worth it. Because I'm worth it! Just as you are as well.

REFLECTION

Do you fear change? If so, when you think about change, what comes up for you? Are you willing to let that old story go in order to have all that you want in this lifetime?

9

LEAVE THE DOOR OPEN

Self Love

Once when I was running,
from all that haunted me.
To the dark I was succumbing -
to what hurt unbearably.
Searching for the one thing,
that would set my sad soul free.
In time I stumbled upon it,
an inner calm and peace;
and now I am beginning,
to see and to believe,
in who I am becoming -
and all I've yet to be.

- Lang Leav

Despite the positive realization that came from my rock bottom moment curled up on the floor, healing doesn't happen overnight. And while I was committed to changing my life, and I was doing the work to make that happen, there were still plenty of times where I slipped up. The difference was that I was getting better at witnessing each mistake instead of allowing them to take me down.

It became a conscious practice, and one that took me some time to embrace and embody fully.

As I've said, my sister was everything to me. And although it's been decades since her death, I still get emotional just talking about her. She was the one person I could count on to be there for me in the good and bad times, never judging me and always loving and accepting me in my beauty and my mess. She never asked for anything from me. Instead, she continued to show up as my big sister, no strings attached. And I, her adoring little sister who loved her fiercely, accepted every part of her in return.

Losing her was devastating for me, but I have continued to hold onto her unconditional love, which has left me with hope throughout the years and has allowed me to pave my own way in the process of rediscovering my truth. Although her death was heartbreaking, at least I had closure. With my sister, there was never a lack of communication or questions left unanswered. We talked about everything, even the hard stuff. I trusted her with my darkness, and I know she felt the same.

But her death, along with my mothers and fathers (and all the other pain I'd endured over the years) taught me that it was best to compartmentalize things, which left me disconnected from the relationships and life that I craved. For so many years, I was emotionally unavailable and found myself slowly drifting away from what little family and friends I had left. I was still waffling in a perpetual cycle of pushing people away when they got too close or I began to feel vulnerable. This pattern, which I had adopted very early on in life, was so deeply ingrained that changing it was downright debilitating and exhausting to navigate as I worked my ass off to heal, once and for all.

For so long I had suppressed my thoughts and subsequently, my emotions, which limited my ability to engage in meaningful relationships. It seemed to be the only way I knew how to cope with the residual, unhealed pain I kept hidden deep inside. I did this in both work and in my personal relationships, a vicious cycle I noticed more so after the death of my sister and my father, in particular. I'd been so used to suppressing, ignoring, and covering up my truth that looking back, I never really understood how to grieve or heal in a healthy and productive way.

While my sister's death was absolutely devastating, it was my father's death that I found the most difficult to process. My father died unexpectedly just a few short years after my sister, and I still had not had the hard conversations to find resolution with him prior to his last breath. I felt a big black hole in my heart after he died, and now it was too late to share how I had felt for most of my life, and give him the opportunity to explain his version of events. The lack of closure became an open wound that I continued to band aid instead of heal, which for years, cost me a tremendous amount of joy and peace.

The wounds of my past became chronically painful. I felt as though I'd been living with a series of puzzle pieces, none of which fit together. Until I could get some answers, I was allowing the questions to continue holding me back, making it impossible for me to fully love myself or anyone else. Not to mention the fact that due to all of the turmoil and confusion, I felt paralyzed when it came to moving forward in every other area of my life as well.

CONFUSION LED CHAOS

Because I felt incomplete, I used this as an excuse when it came to most things, but especially my identity. All of the confusion I felt swirling within my mind and body led me to continue choosing behaviors (and people) that aligned with the pain I felt (that I had not dealt with), instead of the joy I was desperate to experience. Somehow, I still thought that by sharing my heart openly I would be seen as weak, or less than. But the reality was, by hiding the truest parts of myself, I was rejecting any form of love that tried to enter, from myself or those that wanted to support me.

As I've shared, my father and I had somewhat of a confusing relationship. At times, I felt that he loved me (in his own way), like when he would buy me nice things, or use me as a trophy at company parties. And while it was not exactly the kind of expression of love I was seeking, this was "love" as I knew it and eventually, I came to accept that.

But no matter how hard I tried, unconditional love always seemed out of reach. What I later came to realize was that it wasn't that he didn't love me, it was more so that he was only able to show his love the way in which he had received it growing up. I believe that my father lacked a real sense of love and acceptance from his own upbringing, which then translated to the people closest to him - his *chosen* family. My father worked hard, and fought his way to the top. Eventually, he did find success career-wise, which allowed him to receive the accolades and attention he craved as a child. Only it was from his colleagues and peers, not his parents. The love of his immediate family (us) never seemed to be enough. I now know that none of it was personal, it was simply all he knew. At least that's what makes the most sense to me now that I know better and I can look at it all through the eyes of love and compassion.

THE PRICE OF MY FATHERS LOVE

One of my favorite memories of my father was just after my 18th birthday. My family and I went to dinner at one of my father's business colleagues' home, and my father's friend was excited to show my father and myself a car he had for sale in his garage. It was the most beautiful red Mach 151 Mustang I'd ever seen, complete with a sleek black stripe. My young eyes lit up as I walked around the car with my finger sliding along side. I opened the door and sat inside and instantly felt powerful. "You look good in it, Patricia. Your father should buy it for you!" My dad looked at me and saw how enthusiastic I was. "Joe, I will play you for it in a game of pool. If I lose, I will buy it for her. But if I win, it will make for a great conversation over dinner."

Now I knew my father was a pool shark, as he had grown up working and hustling through the pool halls to make money. He'd also taught me how to outplay anyone so I knew there was no way he would possibly lose, which meant there was no way in hell I would be leaving with a new car!

The game was about to begin, and as everyone stood around intensely waiting to see what would happen, the crack of the pool stick against the cue ball was jarring. My dad's friend managed to put a few balls into the pockets before it was my father's turn. And just as I suspected, my father began to run the table. No doubt this would be a short game, as he proceeded to drop the balls in the pockets, over and over again.

And then came the last ball, the 8 ball, which seemed like an easy shot into the side pocket. At this point, I was sure I wasn't going home in that car, and with my head bowed, I started to walk away. Then suddenly, everything changed.

My dad had leaned down to set up his shot, and as he methodically moved the cue ball in the direction of the 8 ball, it became so quiet you could hear your own breath. The last shot had been taken and within an instant people were screaming, "He lost! He actually lost!"

I quickly turned and saw that my father had scratched on the 8 ball. I looked at him in shock, as he stood up with a big Cheshire grin on his face and said, "I guess you just got a new car." I was stunned and knew he had scratched on that 8 ball on purpose, but nothing was ever said. At the end of the night, as I slid into the black bucket seat, I turned on the radio and drove myself home in my brand new, beautiful car all because my father had willingly lost at a game he knew better than most.

I believe that was how he showed his love, although growing up it was incredibly hard for me to wrap my head around. Transactions and business were what he understood, and showing physical hugs or I love you's just was not part of his make up. It was as though showing affection equaled weakness to him, a story that was never spoken, or resolved. I'll never know if my assumptions were true, but his actions led me to believe they were. And in one way or another, choosing to believe he loved me in his own way provides me with a sense of peace.

I held onto these types of memories. Even though they did not bring me closure, they did bring me some comfort. He was gone, and he would never be able to answer my questions directly. But I knew deep inside that my father loved me. He had to, didn't he? I was his daughter, after all.

Over time, and with lots of healing work, I chose to see his form of love as a gift. And because I never received love in the way I felt

I needed, I was committed to working on my own communication with others for I'd realized how important it was that people knew what they meant to you, especially while alive.

I chose to take with me the good things that my father offered, knowing and understanding where he came from and thanking him in my heart for doing what he could for me while he was here. It didn't fix the past, but I decided it would help to heal the pain and direct me towards a better, more loving future.

Growing up and not knowing what love really felt like was confusing at times. I had identified more with fairytales in books then with my own reality. I perceived life with my eyes fixated on fantasy, believing (or hoping) that somehow everything would lead to me having my own happily ever after. My family created a facade to the outside world, where everything appeared perfect and happy. But the truth was, our inner world as a family was toxic and venomous, and far from perfect.

I had learned to wear a mask, and pretend I was fine even when I wasn't. I learned to stay quiet, and not speak up, which meant I had no voice - or at least I had no idea how to use it! For so long, I had been a doormat in my relationships. I let people walk all over me and instead of choosing better, I would run when things got tough and find someone else to do the same thing. I had no compass to guide me when it came to cultivating healthy, sustainable, enjoyable, and loving relationships. When it came to communication, I was clueless! It took me years to understand the importance of being open with my wants, needs and desires, and being brave with my voice, instead of hiding it to appease the masses. It took time, but I finally learned that emotions are not only okay, but healthy and necessary.

I longed to understand love from an emotional place, instead of the materialistic world I'd grown up in. I had seen others seemingly swarming in love, and that meant it was possible. I deeply desired to experience a love like that... a love from the heart and not from possessions.

Despite growing up with a warped sense of love, I believe I am one of the fortunate ones. My mother, who lived a long life, was able to help me bring things full circle before she passed. Something I will forever be grateful for.

In one of our heart-to-heart conversations, years after my fathers death, she shared with me that although it always appeared that she was the one that was standing by my side when I felt lost, confused or found myself traveling down the wrong path, it was actually my father who advised her to keep the door open. He was the one standing behind her with his arms outstretched, not allowing her to shut the door on his little girl. Something I never knew until much later in life.

Hearing this allowed my heart to expand and I truly felt his love, even in his absence. He had loved me after all, and although the way in which he chose to show it was different from what I thought love should look like, he did the best he could with what he knew. His love had always been there, I just didn't have the capacity or understanding to see it at the time.

GRACE IN GRIEF

When I look back on my life, it's clear to me now that I was just being a normal young girl. And like many teens and young adults, I was simply trying to find my way. I didn't have the tools to handle my emotions, or the losses in my life, not to mention all the trauma I experienced first-hand. The only thing I knew to do was to keep going. I skipped over the hard conversations, for fear of appearing weak. I ignored the pain in my heart, choosing resentment and self-loathing instead of seeking to understand and forgive those that really were doing their best. But that was my path, and while it took me decades to choose differently, I wouldn't change a thing. Everything I've been through has served as a gift, and for that, I am beyond blessed.

I believe that every obstacle was divinely placed in my path to encourage my own growth, so that I could support others on their paths someday. I had been seeking love my entire life from others when really, the moment I learned to love myself, I opened the space to feel the love that I had longed for, which had been there all along. I just needed to give myself the grace of being human, and allow it all to flow in.

My life has been a journey, as I'm sure yours has as well. I've taken paths that have led me so far into the depths of despair that I had no choice but to pull myself up off the floor and start over. But there have also been plenty of moments full of joy intertwined in it all.

Life is messy, and often confusing, but it is also full of hope and promise. We don't always see it because at times, the tunnel appears so dark. But what I now know to be true is there is always a light in the darkness and it's up to us to keep going, allowing ourselves to feel and heal along the way while trusting ourselves in the process in order to experience all that's available.

I fought to be where I am today, and I am grateful that I was given the gift of grit and perseverance. Nothing about my life has been easy, but you know what? All of it has been worth it.

REFLECTION

Are you willing to accept that you are a GIFT to this world? By being ALL OF YOU, you are inviting us into your magic, which is the greatest offering anyone could possibly give (or receive) from another human being. Thank you for showing up. Thank you for letting us witness you. Thank you for being so damn brave!

CLOSING

It's not easy going it alone. But if you KEEP GOING, stay true to yourself...
it will be worth it in the end
The hardest walk you can make is the walk you make alone,
but that is the walk that makes you the strongest
That is the walk that builds your character the most
To all of you fighting battles alone, to all of you going against the grain,
battling the naysayers
Stay strong! Keep going!
Stay Strong! Keep going!
This walk is hard, but the hardest walks lead to the greatest destinations
The toughest climbs always lead to the best views
It will be worth it in the end
And if you show what you are made of, the right people will show up in your life
You won't be a lone wolf forever
You have qualities only few can admire, because most don't possess
You have strength only few can understand, because most have never experienced
So don't give in
Don't settle
Don't lower your expectations to fit into the world
You were born to stand out.
You were born to lead.
Lead the pack
They say the wolf on the hill is never as hungry as the wolf climbing the hill
Always be that wolf, climbing the hill
Always hungry for more!

PATRICIA LOVE

Always hungry to grow, to feed your mind and to rise
to the highest level you can take yourself
Never looking back
Always looking forward, to the next feast, Feast of success, in whatever you do
It doesn't matter if you have to walk alone for a while
It is much better to walk alone in the right direction, than to follow
the herd walking in the wrong direction
Stay strong!
Be different!
Your destiny is in your hands!
Get out there and hunt it!

- Fearless Motivation

I sit here today, wearing my bright red lipstick proudly. Not as a cover up, but as a reminder of what I went through and overcame. Basically, because I'm really fucking proud of myself for turning my life around on that particular September day, and for deciding at that very moment that it was time to begin to really, truly love myself. Knowing what I know now, I'm certain that nothing would have changed if I hadn't radically transformed myself, from the inside out. To this day, deciding to take my power back continues to be the best thing I've ever done for myself.

Other than the decision itself, nothing leading up to that decision was easy. Choosing to get brutally honest with myself and diving into the shit was wildly uncomfortable, and confronting. But I knew I didn't have much of a choice if I wanted to live - which I did!

I started by acknowledging all the blessings in my life, and choosing to be grateful for every experience and person as well as my strength to persevere and overcome. I sold everything I could in order to pay off my debt, teaching myself about money in the process so that I could become financially free. I then did the work to forgive myself for any, and all of the mistakes that I had made. And then I forgave all the people that I was still holding onto negative feelings about. This included my parents, rapists, ex-husbands, ex-coworkers,

92

and strangers I'd come into contact with over the decades. It was time to stop playing the victim, and reclaim my life and it was up to me to make that happen.

By letting go of my expectations of others, and not trying to control the outcomes, I was able to become good friends with my second ex-husband. I chose to live in a mindset of hope, faith, and embrace the truth that I was enough - I always have been. I finally believed whole-heartedly that I was capable of overcoming anything when I put my mind to it. Something I've proven to myself over and over again.

When I finally made the decision to hold myself accountable for what I said and did every day, including not allowing men to take advantage of my mind and body any longer, my self-worth skyrock-eted, and my confidence revealed itself. I actually think that was the first time I can honestly say I believed that I was in charge of my own power, and my ability to cultivate the life I'd always envisioned.

By truly loving myself first, I opened my heart and allowed people to love me back. Choosing to be more vulnerable allowed me to step into a fulfilling and joyful life, instead of operating in my old story of, *when (this happens) then love will show up.*

These last several years have been full of change, stretching myself, tears, confusion, uncertainty and lots of uncomfortable moments, none of which have been quick or easy, nor has it always been straightforward. But all of it has absolutely been worth it and necessary for me to grow.

For so long, I carried my suitcase of self-doubt around. When in reality, the little girl within, just as the grown-up me now, has always been worthy simply because I exist. Just as you reading this now are as well.

It was only when I gained the courage necessary to open that suitcase, unpack my past pain, fears, and old stories, and remove anything that was no longer serving the woman I'd become that I was able to love and accept myself, fully and unconditionally. Now that little girl feels empowered and optimistic and the woman I am now smiles knowing that each day is a new day to start again. Even when it feels scary or shitty to do so.

When I first committed to writing this book, I'll admit that I was scared. I questioned myself, "Who am I to share my story?" I thought about what it might mean to show up so vulnerable to the world, opening myself up to criticism, haters, naysayers, and possibly bullies, as I willingly invited strangers, family, friends and clients alike into my private world.

What I realize now is that being brave and saying yes to telling my story has just been another step on my healing journey, and by choosing courage, I continue to show the little girl within that it is safe to be authentic and radically vulnerable in my truth. And also, that her voice (and mine) have always been worthy of being heard.

Maybe you resonate with one or more of my stories throughout these pages. Or maybe you know of someone that might relate. Either way, I want you to know and understand that choosing to be vulnerable and change my life is something that anyone can do, including you. And yes, you are worth the time and effort it takes to create positive change and live the best life possible.

I pushed past my fear and pulled up my big girl pants so I could share my journey and help you unpack your own baggage so that you could take your power back. I hope it's served you well.

I want you to realize that you are enough, and worthy of everything you desire. You are pretty enough, smart enough, capable enough, all of the *enough* to do anything you choose to do. It's time to put that heavy bag down, and unpack it so you can feel and enjoy the world the way you deserve to. It's time for your voice to be heard because the world is waiting to hear it. And you matter.

It's time to stop settling in life, and instead, choose to live life out loud, in your fullest expression possible. You are far more powerful than you may think, and my hope is that this book has helped inspire you to come home to yourself and believe that it's all possible for you too.

Don't give up on your hopes and dreams, or beat yourself up when you make mistakes. We are all flawed, and that's part of what makes us all uniquely beautiful.

Leave the shit in the past, and keep moving forward in your life. Mistakes do not define you. If anything, they make you better.

Don't be afraid that you're too old to change or that your goals are too big or too crazy or too scary. I want you to go for it, and take a chance on YOU! Become a role model for your family, and friends. Be the beginning of the ripple effect that ignites more love, like a stone being thrown as it dances atop the water.

When the going gets tough, pull up your big girl pants and keep moving forward. You can, and you will, succeed. You deserve to release any guilt or shame you may have and learn to forgive yourself. You are human, and being human is messy. Own it. And learn to love it all anyway.

I want you to celebrate all your wins and your losses, and embrace life's cycles. Communicate and appreciate every little moment with your loved ones, as we never know when they will be gone. You deserve to achieve inner peace and happiness, and I promise you… it's available. Yes, even for you.

You deserve to cultivate more presence in your busy life so you can become calmer, kinder, happier and more relaxed, and learn to make room for those "take your breath away" moments.

The best gift you can give to others is your Presence.

I want you to believe that a real, healthy partnership means growing together, and realize that everything has its ups and down. Even love. I also want you to understand that real strength lies in working through the tough times together, and coming out stronger on the other side.

Have faith in Love.

I want you to feel and welcome your power from within and develop a deep sense of worth and knowing when it comes to money, sex, intimacy, and relationships of all kinds.

You were born Enough.

Will this be hard in today's culture? Yes! It takes courage to take the steps necessary to make these things a reality. But you are not doing anyone any favors by compromising your truth or your values to fit into someone else's box. It's time to build your own beautiful home with windows and doors, letting the light shine in no matter what storms come your way. Change is a process, often a messy one. But it's also a beautiful thing, if you allow it to be.

I will not promise ease. But I can promise possibility. And you're worth fighting for!

To get you started, there are five activities and actions I recommend:

#1 - Start. Seems so simple, right? And it can be. So many people begin, only to quit. But not you. Tomorrow is not promised, so there's no better time than now to write a new story.

Don't worry about having a grandiose plan. Don't be that person that says, "I will do it tomorrow." This is your life, and your life doesn't start tomorrow, your life is happening right now. So saddle up and get ready for the ride of your life!

#2 - Love Yourself. I love this part of my daily practice - mirror work. By doing the mirror exercise every night before you go to bed, you're giving your inner child (who lives in your subconscious mind) the positive reinforcement she needs to move forward towards positive achievements. We all need some form of acknowledgment, and the most important acknowledgement is the acknowledgment you give yourself.

Stand in front of the mirror before you go to bed and celebrate everything you accomplished that day, addressing yourself by name. Get into the habit of appreciating yourself out loud.

For Example:

- Any personal disciplines you kept; dietary, exercise, reading mediation, spiritual or prayer
- Any achievements; business, financial, educational, personal, physical, spiritual or emotional
- Any temptations that you did *not* give into; watching too much TV, staying up too late, drinking, smoking etc.

When looking in the mirror, make sure you look yourself straight in the eyes. It may be a bit uncomfortable at first, but do it anyway. After you have finished openly appreciating yourself, look deep into your eyes and tell yourself, "I love you" - without running away!

Choose the discomfort and stay committed to the process of change. Allow yourself to feel the impact of this practice.

The most important piece of this exercise is not to pull away or run if feelings of embarrassment (or the like) come up. You may find yourself judging this exercise, or yourself, but this is not why we're here. I get that this may feel silly, but most of us were never taught to appreciate ourselves, and it's something that is so powerful to master! Even if it feels uncomfortable at first, keep going. Whatever you do, don't give up. In about 21-30 days you will begin to see the negative self-talk lessen and your confidence begin to rise.

This is a must do exercise. It's the start of retraining your mind, and loving yourself on a soul level. And look at it this way, if you do it tonight you will have something to appreciate tomorrow night, and all the nights after. I still do this every day and I'm telling you, it works!

#3 - Keep Going. One of the hardest things to do is to keep going, refusing to give up! I know it probably sucks to hear, but there are some people that may very well love to see you fail, even your own inner critic. If you start to waffle or think about quitting, I want you to do the following instead...

#4 - Come Back To Your Why. Really think about why you are doing this in the first place... Why are you ready and willing to change? Why is this so important (and likely, necessary) to your overall, long-term happiness? Your why should be so strong that nothing, I mean *nothing*, will stop you from staying the course. Dig within and find a big enough reason to stick to it, and not lose interest. Make it powerful! Having a strong why as your foundation is critical to get you through the tough times. We are all different. We hold different values, come from different backgrounds, have different beliefs. So your WHY has to be something that will truly drive you, nobody else.

Write it down and keep it in a place where you can revisit it often. Read it out loud every morning, and every night if you must! Whatever you need to do to keep going!

When you have your WHY, you will be unstoppable!

#5 - Quietation. This is not meditation, let's get that straight. This is a "timeout" - quiet time just for you to reconnect to yourself, your why, and your path. How many times have you given your kids a time out? Well, think of this as an adult time out - a critical activity that will change your life once you START.

I want you to take 5 minutes and slowly build up to 30 minutes a day to *just be*. Be quiet, open your heart and focus on yourself, your breath, your thoughts, and your dreams. This is essential in order to get clarity in your life and what you're creating. Block off 5 minutes (or more) daily in your calendar, working your way up to 30 minutes (or more) each day.

Your mind will become so focused, you will create more energy, more opportunities, and you will be a better problem solver.

Without quietation in your life, it's hard to change. You must take the time and clear your mind, to allow your creativity and ideas to flow. When you let the quiet in, your soul becomes clear.

YOU'RE DOING GREAT!

Take the time to go back through the previous chapters and work through the questions as you feel called. I'm willing to bet that you will learn something new about yourself each time.

And while the stories within this book may have been mine, I want to reiterate that I chose to share them with you to provide you with a sense of hope and remind you that no matter what your current situation, any past behaviors, or moments that you have gone through, you can change your life. You deserve to live your best life... and live it to the fullest!

And last, but certainly not least, trust yourself. I know that you can do this. I believe in you and it's time that you believe in you, too.